C000128456

Brittany (B Guide: Cancale, Carnac, Dinan, Morlaix, Paimpont, Brocéliande Forest, Perros-Guirec, Quiberon, Quimper, Josselin, Vannes

Explore Roscoff, Carantec, Brest, Dinard in France

Hudson Miles

This travel guide provides helpful information. If you're interested in knowing about the city's attractions, accommodation options, transportation, leisure activities, restaurants, shopping, and many more, there are recommended options in this book with their contact details. For first-timers, visiting or contacting the Tourist office helps you get familiar with the city and its attractions.

Check out the section of Practical Tips to know more about France, or go for my book 'France Travel Tips' and explore other cities in France and Italy.

Lastly, try the travel prompts; they help enrich your travel experience and open avenues for personal growth.

Safe Trip

Scan the QR code below, if interested in booking your accommodation online.

Table Of Contents

Brittany

Located in northwest France, the large peninsula of Brittany boasts an extensive coastline. Because of its large parks and woods, history, and culture, it is a well-liked travel destination for both French and foreign tourists.

There is much for everyone in Brittany, or Breizh in Breton. The Neolithic era is represented by the enormous standing stones, or menhirs, found in Carnac and the surrounding area. The rows of standing stones recall the first inhabitants of Brittany; some of them are even older than Stonehenge.

Situated a short distance south of Carnac, the picturesque Quiberon Peninsula boasts untamed beaches and jagged cliffs, an abundance of hiking trails, and a few small towns complete with lodging and dining options. It is also an important centre for seafood, and boats to nearby islands leave from its little harbour.

From Carnac, head northeast to Vannes, a quaint mediaeval port town with distinctive architecture and winding alleyways. Travel south to see the Château of the Dukes of Brittany at Nantes, the largest city in mediaeval Brittany. Then head north into the woodlands to Josselin, a small village overshadowed by its majestic château.

Even further north lies Quimper, the capital of the Finistère (Land's End) region. Quimper is renowned for its exquisite and unique hand-glazed ceramics, or faience. Quimper is also a hub of Breton culture, with bilingual signage in French and Breton describing the main sights.
Finistère also includes the Crozon Peninsula, which offers stunning hiking trails and views of the rocky coastline. The harbour city of Brest is about to the north. A tiny town called Morlaix lies farther inland. It has a huge railway viaduct and makes a great starting point for exploring the numerous parish closures in this area. North of Morlaix, Roscoff is connected to Britain and Ireland by boat.

Guimiliau's gorgeous parish, close by, in Brittany. There are about 200 carved figurines in the Calvary!

East of Finistére in the Brittany department of Côtes d'Armor, the quaint beach village of Perros-Guirec is well-known for its red granite cliffs and its proximity to the Sentier des Douaniers, the region's well-known walking trail. A few World War II sites are also present, including the little village of Plouha.

Mont St. Michel is situated close to the Brittany border, even though it is officially in Normandy. Easily reachable from Rennes, the provincial capital of Brittany, is Mont St-Michel.

Situated near Rennes and Mont St-Michel, St-Malo is a corsair village on the northern coast of Brittany. The fortified city of St. Malo is a beautiful place to come if you want to take in the history and seashore. Across the harbour is the 19th-century tourist town of Dinard. A mere 24 km south on the Rance River lies a place called Dinan; do not confuse it with Dinard. Ramparts enclose the quaint mediaeval town of Dinan.

Check my book on Saint-Malo

St. Malo's National Fort

We saw views of St. Malo's Fort National from our hotel room. When the tide comes in, even though you went there during low tide, it turns into an island!

Cancale is a fishing village around 15 km (9 miles) from St-Malo and 50 km (31 miles) from Mont St-Michel, if you want oysters.

Regarding cuisine, Brittany is a gourmet haven! Not only is Brittany famous for its mussels, cider, and crêpes, but it also produces delicious pastries and other treats.

Throughout its history, Brittany has changed, and it was formerly a sovereign nation. Its language reflects how important its Celtic heritage is. The unique history of this French province is reflected in its folk music, which has experienced a rebirth in recent decades.
There is also a great deal of mythology, including stories about Merlin and King Arthur. There's even "Merlin's tomb" in Brocéliande.

Kouign-amann
(Bread and butter)

Cuisines

Classic Breton specialties, crêpes (sweet) and galettes (savoury), are served in many restaurants and are frequently distributed as street snacks. They are located throughout Paris and other parts of France, as well as in Brittany and Normandy, where they may provide a delicious dinner at a reasonable price.

Because of its long coastline, Brittany is also renowned for its delicious seafood. Savour delicious freshly shucked oysters or moules frites (mussels served with fries or chips) for lunch or dinner.

Seafood is a common pairing for Nantes-region mussad wine.

The typical drinks of Brittany include strong apple brandy called Calvados and slightly frothy cider. There's also an assortment of apéritifs, many with a cider base.

Then there come the sweets and desserts. The classic kouign amann is a fantastic pastry made with butter, flour, and sugar. Layers of dough are formed by the incorporation of butter and sugar into the crust, and during baking, the sugar turns caramel.

For snacking, patisseries sell individual tiny ones as well as large ones. How on earth could you say no? After going through a number of stores in St. Malo.

Delicious! Another highlight of the area is a Far Breton, which is a deep custard similar to clafouti that usually has prunes in it. Due to its ease of preparation and lack of sweetness, the Far is a well-liked meal in Brittany.

Travelling is a cultural experience, and I think that seeing and enjoying the local cuisine and drink—which you can compare to the food and drink of Normandy—is an integral part of it.

Savour the delicious and distinctive Breton cuisine and beverages!

French Phrases and slang terms

Basic french phrases and area slang terms to know before travelling.

- Bonjour - Hello
- Merci - Thank you
- S'il vous plaît - Please
- Excusez-moi - Excuse me
- Oui - Yes
- Non - No
- Comment ça va ? - How are you?
- Bien, merci - Fine, thank you
- Au revoir - Goodbye
- Bonsoir - Good evening
- Bonne nuit - Good night
- Comment vous appelez-vous ? - What is your name?
- Je m'appelle... - My name is...
- Enchanté(e) - Nice to meet you
- Où est... ? - Where is...?
- Combien ça coûte ? - How much does it cost?
- L'addition, s'il vous plaît - The bill, please
- Pouvez-vous m'aider ? - Can you help me?
- Excusez-moi, où sont les toilettes ? - Excuse me, where are the toilets?
- J'ai besoin d'une assistance médicale - I need medical assistance
- Pouvez-vous parler plus lentement ? - Can you speak more slowly?

- Pouvez-vous répéter, s'il vous plaît ? - Can you repeat, please?
- Quand est l'heure du départ ? - When is the departure time?
- Où puis-je acheter des billets ? - Where can I buy tickets?
- J'aimerais réserver une chambre - I would like to book a room
- Avez-vous une chambre disponible ? - Do you have a room available?
- Quel est le mot pour... en français ? - What is the word for... in French?
- Pouvez-vous recommander un bon restaurant ? - Can you recommend a good restaurant?
- Quel est le plat du jour ? - What is the dish of the day?
- Où puis-je trouver un taxi ? - Where can I find a taxi?
- Pouvez-vous m'indiquer le chemin vers... ? - Can you show me the way to...?
- Avez-vous du wifi ici ? - Do you have wifi here?
- J'ai une réservation - I have a reservation
- C'est délicieux ! - It's delicious!
- Où puis-je prendre le bus ? - Where can I take the bus?
- Quelle est la météo aujourd'hui ? - What is the weather like today?
- Avez-vous des recommandations touristiques ? - Do you have any sightseeing recommendations?
- C'est magnifique ! - It's beautiful!
- Où puis-je trouver un distributeur automatique ? - Where can I find an ATM?
- J'ai perdu mon chemin - I'm lost

- Avez-vous un plan de la ville ? - Do you have a city map?
- Pouvez-vous me recommander un bon café ? - Can you recommend a good café?
- Pouvez-vous me donner l'heure ? - Can you tell me the time?
- Où puis-je acheter des souvenirs ? - Where can I buy souvenirs?
- Je voudrais essayer quelque chose de typique - I would like to try something typical
- Pouvez-vous me recommander une bonne boulangerie ? - Can you recommend a good bakery?
- C'est vraiment intéressant ! - That's really interesting!
- Où puis-je louer un vélo ? - Where can I rent a bike?
- Quel est le moyen de transport le plus rapide ? - What is the fastest mode of transportation?
- Y a-t-il des visites guidées disponibles ? - Are there guided tours available?
- Pouvez-vous m'indiquer le chemin vers la gare ? - Can you show me the way to the train station?
- Pouvez-vous me donner un conseil de voyage ? - Can you give me a travel tip?
- Avez-vous des informations touristiques ? - Do you have tourist information?
- J'ai besoin d'un adaptateur électrique - I need an electrical adapter
- Quelle est la meilleure période pour visiter ? - What is the best time to visit?
- Pouvez-vous me recommander un bon livre en français ? - Can you recommend a good book in French?
- J'ai une allergie alimentaire - I have a food allergy

- Où puis-je trouver un supermarché ? - Where can I find a supermarket?
- Pouvez-vous me recommander un bon vin local ? - Can you recommend a good local wine?
- Où puis-je prendre le métro ? - Where can I take the subway?
- Y a-t-il un musée près d'ici ? - Is there a museum nearby?
- J'ai besoin d'un médecin - I need a doctor
- Pouvez-vous me recommander un bon endroit pour faire du shopping ? - Can you recommend a good place for shopping?
- C'est très gentil de votre part - That's very kind of you
- Pouvez-vous m'aider à trouver un hôtel abordable ? - Can you help me find an affordable hotel?
- Où puis-je trouver un bureau de change ? - Where can I find a currency exchange office?
- J'ai besoin d'un taxi pour l'aéroport - I need a taxi to the airport
- Où puis-je louer une voiture ? - Where can I rent a car?
- C'est une belle journée ! - It's a beautiful day!
- Y a-t-il des événements spéciaux en ce moment ? - Are there any special events happening now?
- Pouvez-vous me recommander une belle plage ? - Can you recommend a beautiful beach?
- C'est une expérience inoubliable ! - It's an unforgettable experience!
- J'ai oublié mon passeport - I forgot my passport
- Quel est le code wifi ? - What is the wifi code?
- C'est vraiment impressionnant ! - It's really impressive!

- Où puis-je trouver un bon endroit pour écouter de la musique live ? - Where can I find a good place to listen to live music?
- Pouvez-vous me donner des informations sur les horaires de transport en commun ? - Can you provide information on public transportation schedules?
- C'est vraiment pratique ! - That's really convenient!
- Pouvez-vous me recommander un bon endroit pour faire de la randonnée ? - Can you recommend a good place for hiking?
- J'ai besoin d'un service de blanchisserie - I need laundry service
- Où puis-je acheter des billets pour des attractions touristiques ? - Where can I buy tickets for tourist attractions?
- Pouvez-vous me recommander un bon restaurant végétarien ? - Can you recommend a good vegetarian restaurant?
- C'est incroyable ! - It's amazing!
- Pouvez-vous me donner des informations sur les horaires d'ouverture des magasins ? - Can you provide information on store opening hours?
- J'ai réservé une visite guidée - I booked a guided tour
- Pouvez-vous me recommander un bon endroit pour prendre des photos ? - Can you recommend a good place for taking photos?
- C'est vraiment délicieux ! - It's really tasty!
- Pouvez-vous me recommander un bon endroit pour voir le coucher du soleil ? - Can you recommend a good place to see the sunset?

- J'ai besoin d'une connexion internet stable - I need a stable internet connection
- Où puis-je trouver un distributeur de billets ? - Where can I find an ATM?
- Pouvez-vous me recommander un bon endroit pour goûter des spécialités locales ? - Can you recommend a good place to try local specialties?
- C'est une belle vue ! - It's a beautiful view!
- Pouvez-vous me donner des informations sur les horaires des trains ? - Can you provide information on train schedules?
- J'ai réservé une chambre pour deux nuits - I booked a room for two nights
- Pouvez-vous me recommander un bon endroit pour pratiquer des sports nautiques ? - Can you recommend a good place for water sports?
- C'est vraiment relaxant ! - It's really relaxing!
- Pouvez-vous me donner des conseils sur la sécurité ? - Can you give me safety tips?
- Où puis-je trouver un bon endroit pour faire du shopping de souvenirs ? - Where can I find a good place for souvenir shopping?
- Pouvez-vous me recommander un bon endroit pour faire du ski ? - Can you recommend a good place for skiing?
- C'est une expérience unique ! - It's a unique experience!
- Pouvez-vous me donner des informations sur les horaires des ferries ? - Can you provide information on ferry schedules?

- J'ai réservé une table pour deux personnes - I booked a table for two
- Pouvez-vous me recommander un bon endroit pour observer les étoiles ? - Can you recommend a good place for stargazing?
- C'est vraiment intéressant de découvrir la culture locale ! - It's really interesting to explore the local culture!
- Pouvez-vous me donner des informations sur les horaires des bus ? - Can you provide information on bus schedules?
- J'ai besoin d'un service de navette pour l'aéroport - I need shuttle service to the airport
- Pouvez-vous me recommander un bon endroit pour visiter des châteaux ? - Can you recommend a good place to visit castles?
- C'est une ville charmante ! - It's a charming city!
- Pouvez-vous me donner des informations sur les horaires des vols ? - Can you provide information on flight schedules?
- J'ai réservé une excursion d'une journée - I booked a day trip
- Pouvez-vous me recommander un bon endroit pour faire du vélo ? - Can you recommend a good place for cycling?
- C'est vraiment spectaculaire ! - It's truly spectacular!
- Pouvez-vous me donner des informations sur les horaires des visites guidées ? - Can you provide information on guided tour schedules?
- J'ai besoin d'un endroit pour charger mon téléphone - I need a place to charge my phone

- Pouvez-vous me recommander un bon endroit pour faire de la plongée ? - Can you recommend a good place for diving?
- C'est une expérience culinaire unique ! - It's a unique culinary experience!
- Pouvez-vous me donner des informations sur les horaires des fermetures des attractions touristiques ? - Can you provide information on closing times for tourist attractions?
- J'ai réservé une croisière - I booked a cruise
- Pouvez-vous me recommander un bon endroit pour admirer l'architecture locale ? - Can you recommend a good place to admire local architecture?
- C'est vraiment captivant ! - It's truly captivating!

Slang terms

- Breizh - Slang term for Brittany, derived from the Breton language name for the region.
- P'tit dej - Abbreviation for "petit déjeuner," meaning breakfast.
- Crêpe-party - Refers to a gathering or party where crêpes are the main food.
- Blé noir - Slang for buckwheat, a key ingredient in savory Breton crêpes.
- Binious - Traditional Breton bagpipes, often used in folk music.
- P'tit Lu - Slang for a person from Nantes, referring to the popular French biscuit brand.
- Fest-noz - Traditional Breton dance party or night festival.

- Kig ha farz - Traditional Breton dish, a type of pork stew with buckwheat pudding.
- Chouchen - Breton honey mead, a popular local alcoholic beverage.
- Armor - Slang for the coastal areas of Brittany.
- Argoat - Slang for the inland, wooded areas of Brittany.
- Cidre - Breton cider, a common local beverage.
- Triskel - Symbolic triple spiral often associated with Breton culture.
- Pardon - Local festival or religious procession.
- Plouc - Slang for someone from a rural area, equivalent to "hick" in English.
- Gavé - Expression meaning "a lot" or "too much."
- Biniou-biniou - Informal term for a small, lightweight boat.
- Plouk - Similar to "plouc," referring to someone from a rural or less urban area.
- Baraques à frites - Slang for places selling French fries, often associated with beachside stalls.
- P'tite mousse - Slang for a small beer, often used when ordering a small glass.
- C'est le bazar - Expression meaning "it's a mess" or "it's chaotic."
- Pochon - Slang for a small bag or pouch.
- Glouglou - Informal term for wine, referring to the sound of pouring.
- Bordel - Expression used for chaos or disorder, equivalent to "mess" in English.
- Bretonnant - Someone who speaks the Breton language.

- Baraqué - Slang for someone who is strong or muscular.
- Binouse - Slang for a beer, often used casually when ordering one.
- Breizh cola - Local Breton cola brand, popular as an alternative to major cola brands.
- C'est canon - Expression meaning "it's great" or "awesome."
- Varech - Seaweed, sometimes used in regional dishes.
- Trogne - Slang for face or expression, similar to "mug" in English.
- Tantad - Breton traditional bonfire celebration.
- Bistrot - A small, cozy bar or pub, often serving traditional Breton dishes.
- Breton bleu - Slang for a local Breton cheese.
- Chnok - Slang for a small, insignificant amount.
- Korrigan - Mythical creature from Breton folklore, similar to leprechauns.
- Plouf - Onomatopoeia for the sound of something falling into water, used humorously.
- Charette - Slang for a small cart or wagon.
- Fanch - Slang for a local Breton sailor.
- Gouel - Breton festival or celebration.
- Binz - Slang for something chaotic or confusing.

Cancale

Cancale is a charming little beach village on the point of a peninsula in Brittany, near St-Malo. It has a lovely setting, and the views of the town as you approach from the south are breathtaking.

Several modest, atmospheric hotels and guesthouses along the beachfront, and others are just a short distance inland.

Cancale is well-known for its oyster beds, which are located immediately offshore. Visitors go to its waterfront restaurants to eat fresh oysters and other seafood. It's ideal for an afternoon stroll or a lunch stop on the way between St-Malo (15 km/9 miles) and Mont-St-Michel (50 km/31 miles).

The most exciting way to eat oysters is to get them fresh from one of the vendors at the little market area near the Fenêtre Jetty, which is located at the end of the major waterfront boulevard. Choose the size and amount you want (plates hold a dozen) and wait while they are opened. Take your plate to the sea wall, take a seat, and dig in, discarding the empty shells. Delicious!

At low tide, you can see the oyster beds. If you gaze further out, you can see Mont-St-Michel in the distance. If you're truly into oysters, Cancale even has an oyster museum. The upper town, located on a hill above the port, features a beautiful church and other monuments.

The harbour is bordered with parking lots, which fill up quickly on a sunny weekend. Find a parking spot and then stroll down to the jetty to sample the oysters. There are eateries all around the waterfront if you prefer a sit-down lunch.

Consider a quick excursion after lunch to the adjacent Pointe du Grouin, a stunning panoramic waterfront park a few kilometres north of Cancale.

Cancale tourist information centre, 44 Rue du Port,
35260 Cancale, France
Phone: +33 2 99 56 66 99

Hotels
Half of Cancale's hotels are located along the seafront in the town centre, where they are close to the sea, seafood restaurants, and water views.
Other hotels are located inland, some only a few minutes' walk away, while others require a short drive.

Consider the 3-star, 16-room Le Continental, located directly on Quai Thomas in the heart of the bustle and near to the oyster beds. Naturally, its restaurant, L'Ormeau, specialises in seafood.
Not far away is the 3-star, 10-room Le Cancalais, which also has its own restaurant.

Marie Galante is a 19th-century stone fisherman's house that has been turned into a four-person vacation rental. The beach is only 30 metres (33 yards) away.

- Hôtel Restaurant de la Pointe du Grouin - Pointe du Grouin - Tel: +33 2 99 89 60 55
  Elegant hotel with comfortable sea-view accommodations, superb restaurants, and free Wi-Fi.

- Brit Hotel Cancale Alghotel - 61 Av. du Général de Gaulle - Tél: +33 2 99 89 50 00

Modern, unassuming hotel with spa, rooftop patio, and sunloungers.

- Hôtel Duguay-Trouin – 11 Quai Duguay Trouin – Phone: +33 2 23 15 12 07

Sea-themed rooms, whirlpool spas, and a relaxed coastal guesthouse with a breakfast terrace are available.

- Le Continental - Phone: +33 2 99 89 60 16 - Address: 4 Quai Admis en Chef Thomas

Rooms are casual, with some having balconies overlooking the port, Wi-Fi, and a seafood restaurant.

- La Maison de Lucile - 3 Avenue de Scissy - Phone: +33 2 99 89 75 59

Uncomplicated rooms with kitchenettes, an outdoor pool, and a spa area in a relaxed hotel.

- Le Chatellier - Phone: +33 2 99 89 81 84 - Location: Les Douets Fleuris

Rooms in an unassuming rural hotel with an outdoor pool, parking, and Wi-Fi.

Grouin's Point

Pointe du Grouin is about a 5-kilometer (3-mile) drive from the seaside resort of Cancale.

It is situated on a rocky outcrop with views east over the Bay of Mont-St-Michel, north towards Jersey, and west across the northern coast of Brittany towards St-Malo.

The stunning blue water contrasts with the rocks and foliage, and the steep cliffs contribute to the dramatic appeal.

You can explore the area by walking routes (but be mindful of the tides).

At Pointe du Grouin, you can witness a variety of sea birds and maybe even a dolphin or two. At the Pointe du Grouin, there is also a small restaurant/hotel.

Restaurants

Hotel Restaurant de la Pointe du Grouin Phone: +33 2 99 89 60 55 Address: Pointe du Grouin, 35260 Cancale, France

La Table de Breizh - 6 Quai Admis en Chef Thomas - Tél: +33 2 99 89 56 46

Japanese food by the water, serving sushi, tempura, and teppanyaki in an attractive setting.

L'Ormeau - Phone: +33 2 99 89 60 16 - Location: Quai Admis en Chef Thomas

A lovely restaurant with a bay view that serves French dishes as well as seafood and regional specialties.

A Contre Courant Cancale Restaurant - 3 Pl. du Calvaire - Phone: +33 2 99 89 61 61

Fresh oysters, bouillabaisse, and escargot are available on the waterfront terrace.

Le Bout du Quai – Route de la Corniche – Phone: +33 2 23 15 13 62

Modern French fare with inventive delicacies such as duck confit, coq au vin, and tarte tatin.

L'Atelier de l'Huitre Restaurant - 15 Quai Gambetta - Phone: +33 2 23 15 13 76

A French-inspired seafood restaurant with oyster specialties, bouillabaisse, and crème brûlée.

Kouign-amann
(Bread and butter)

Shopping:

While in the city, make sure to visit these recommended shops for a memorable shopping experience. You can bring back some souvenirs from your trip.

Une Journée à la Mer - Type: Gift Shop - Location: 28 Quai Gambetta - Phone: +33 2 99 80 74 36
Charming seaside gift shop with unusual seashore souvenirs and marine-themed treasures.

Bazar Parisien - Address: 42 Rue du Port - Phone: +33 2 99 89 62 97 - Type: Discount store
Budget-friendly bargain retailer that sells everything from household necessities to stylish accessories.

Cancale City Centre Market
- Category: Grocery Store - Location: 2 Rue de la Marine
Fresh fruit, regional delicacies, and daily necessities are available at this town centre grocery store.

HUBLOT Mode Marine
- Category: Clothing Store - Location: 2 Quai Gambetta - Phone: +33 2 23 15 65 11
Fashionable clothing boutique with a nautical motif, offering fashionable clothing for a coastal wardrobe.

Leisure Activities:

Here are some more activities and excursions in the city or nearby to get involved in:

Segway Ride in Saint-Malo - Saint-Malo Entertainment - Price: €29 to €45 - Explore Saint-Malo in a playful way with Gyromalo, covering 13 kilometres. Sylvain will show you hidden gems and Malouine heritage.

Bay of Saint-Malo Cruise with Commentary - Culture and education in Saint-Malo - Price: €23 - Discover the Emerald Coast since 1904 with regular lines and a Bay of Saint-Malo cruise, located 13.2 kilometres away.

Private Cruise from Pointe du Grouin to Cap Fréhel - Nature and the great outdoors in Saint-Malo - Price: €160 to €400 - Enjoy sea walks on the Emerald Coast with a private boat for up to 7 people, 13.6 kilometres distant.

Dinard Saint-Malo Vedette Boat Crossing - Nature and the great outdoors in Dinard - Price: €8 - Explore the North Brittany Coast with regular line crossings, including Saint-Malo/Dinard, located 15.4 kilometres away.

Attend an Exhibition and Sale at Dol-de-Bretagne Artists' Studios - Arts and Crafts
    - Cost: free - 15.8 kilometres distant, discover the creativity of painters in Dol-de-Bretagne. From April 1st to October 15th, discover regional artistic and artisanal skills.

Festivals and Events:
Attending the events listed below in the city or nearby can make your trip memorable.

Every Sunday morning, the Cancale market is held. In December, there is also a Christmas market. During the summer, a night market is held on Thursdays from 5 p.m. until 8 p.m. In July, there will also be a clearance sale.

In March, the Cancale Challenges walking race is held. The trip is somewhat more than ten kilometres long.

The Mont-Saint-Michel Bay Marathon begins near the port of La Houle in Cancale at the end of May. You can choose from three different events and distances.

The Grouin festival, held in early June, is a theatre event geared towards young people. Children and teenagers perform plays on stage for the occasion.

Le Branle-Bas de Régates is a maritime festival held in August with various activities for people of all ages. Several ports from Mont Saint-Michel to Saint-Malo participate in these nautical events.

The Cancale Bordées festival, held between the end of September and the beginning of October, features a variety of performances of traditional marine music in cafes, gardens, the streets, and beneath a cabaret marquee.

Carnac

Carnac is a little Breton village near the Golfe du Morbihan, not far from the beautiful Quiberon Peninsula.

Carnac is a little town with a lengthy history. Around Carnac, over 3000 megalithic monuments dating from the fifth to the third millennium BC are grouped in various formations. These alignments, known as menhirs, which means "long stone" in Breton, are really stunning.

Although there are currently 3000 stones left, researchers believe there were twice that many in prehistory. They were put to many uses over the centuries. "Every house in Carnac has a menhir," our guide said during our visit to the Kermario Alignments.

Carnac has three major megalithic sites, as well as several lesser sites, all of which are easily accessible. The Ménec Alignments are directly across the road from the Visitors' Centre. It Comprises 1050 stones scattered throughout 950 metres.
The Kermario Alignments, the most visited and largest megalithic site, are just down the road. At one end, there is also a dolmen, or room.

Kerlescan is a group of 13 rows of menhirs, some of which are quite well maintained. From the road, all of the important attractions are visible.
The Géant du Manio, a six-meter-high megalith set off the road and down a wooded walk, is one of the smaller sites.
Although you could simply roam among the stones when I first visited Carnac this year, erosion and other damage has resulted in programmes to conserve the stones and the plants surrounding them. Major sites are visited with the assistance of a guide (information available at the Visitors' Centre), who ensures that visitors do not harm the environment. Tours are available in French, English, German, and other languages during the season.
So, what did these stones serve? They are arranged in rows, with the largest stones facing west and the smallest facing east. Some believe these may be religious places, and one end looks to be enclosed.

People thought the stones were Celtic or Druidic until the 1950s, when study revealed they were far older. The stones were most likely "repurposed" by the Celts for their own uses.

Despite the age of the stones, Brittany was populated long before they were built. The Prehistoric Museum in Carnac depicts Brittany's history from the Palaeolithic period (450,000 BC) to the Middle Ages. A trip to the museum can help put the stones into context.

If you're looking for Neolithic sites in Brittany, consider visiting the Cairn of Barnenez in the Finistère region. This passage tomb is Europe's largest mausoleum and was built between 4500 and 3900 BCE.

After contemplating antiquity, head to Carnac-Plage or the adjacent (30-minute drive) Quiberon Peninsula for beautiful beaches, cliffs, and hiking paths. You can also drive a half-hour northwest to Vannes, a mediaeval town at the mouth of the Golfe du Morbihan.

Carnac Tourist Information Centre Address: 74 Av. des Druides, 56340 Carnac, France
Hours:
Phone: +33 2 97 52 13 52

Hotels:

When traveling, it's advisable to book your hotel in advance. I recommend using Booking.com for great deals, and it is available for some hotels in any country. Scan the QR code to learn more. Here are some recommended hotels to consider

- Le Plancton - Phone: +33 2 97 52 13 65 - Address: 12 Bd de la Plage

  A simple beach hotel with streamlined rooms, sea-view balconies, and complimentary breakfast.

- Thalazur Carnac - Address: 2 Avenue de l'Atlantique - Phone: +33 2 97 52 53 00

  Hotel featuring 8 tennis courts, an outdoor pool, and a casual restaurant on a lakeside.

- MARINE HOTEL BAR RESTAURANT

- Address: 4 Place de la Chapelle - Phone: +33 2 97 52 07 33

The hotel is unpretentious, with simply furnished rooms, a restaurant/bar, and complimentary Wi-Fi.

- Le Celtique Hôtel & Wellness - Carnac-Plage - Address: 82 Avenue des Druides - Phone: +33 2 97 52 14 15

Relaxed ocean-view rooms in a light-filled hotel with a full-service spa and an attractive indoor pool.

- LE DIANA Hôtel & Spa Nuxe - Address: 21 Boulevard de la Plage - Phone: +33 2 97 52 05 38

Hotel on the beach has basic rooms with balconies, a pool, patio dining and a bustling rum bar.

Restaurants:
For a relaxed and enjoyable dining experience, try any of the following top restaurants. I've included their contact details:

La Potinière - 25 Av. Miln - Charming French restaurant serving escargot and coq au vin in a sociable, global-themed ambiance.

Le Cavok - Address: 22 Av. Miln - Phone: +33 2 97 14 56 08

French cuisine at its finest, with delicacies like bouillabaisse and ratatouille available for dine-in or takeout.

La Sultana - Address: 4 Av. Miln - Phone: +33 2 97 52 28 50

With a beautiful terrace environment, this stylish restaurant and bar serves escargot and duck confit.

La Poêle à Crêpes - 49 Avenue des Druides - Phone: +33 2 97 57 95 35

An old-fashioned crêperie serving classic galettes and sweet crêpes on a gorgeous terrace.

Le 18ème Amendement - Address: 9 All. du Parc - Téléphone: +33 2 97 58 44 41

French bistro with no takeaway, serving boeuf bourguignon and coq au vin.

Chez Auguste Créperie – Lieu-dit, Montauban – Phone: +33 2 97 58 24 84

In a gorgeous café setting, this charming creperie serves delectable galettes and crêpes.

Shopping:
While in the city, make sure to visit these recommended shops for a memorable shopping experience. You can bring back some souvenirs from your trip.

- Les Boutiques De La Plage - Shop: Store - Type: General store - Address: 64 Av. des Druides

- Jolies Bretonnes Carnac - Clothing store - Type: Boutique - Address: 8 All. du Parc - Phone: +33 6 13 33 74 04

- Aux Korrigans - Souvenir store - Type: Gift shop - Address: 1 Pl. de l'Église - Phone: +33 2 97 52 04 29

- Clémentine - Gift shop - Type: Boutique - Address: Avenue de l'atlantique, Place de port a Drô - Phone: +33 2 97 52 96 34

Dinan

Dinan, a lovely mediaeval Breton walled town on a hill overlooking the Rance River, is surrounded by a modern town of about 10,000 people.

The mediaeval city of Vieux Dinan has been wonderfully conserved, with its narrow winding alleyways and half-timbered buildings and stores. Craftsmen who create and sell traditional arts, food, and drink items are given special attention.

The streets will explain why the centre is largely a pedestrian zone. Large parking lots surround the city, both inside and outside the city limits.

The most well-known street is Rue du Jerzual, a winding, tiny lane that leads from the middle of town down to the Rance River port. This street offers numerous views of the buildings and exhibits the town's mediaeval charm.

Sections of the walls remain, and the towers offer stunning views of the town and the river valley. The view of the valley from Ste Catherine's Tower is breathtaking. Visitors can tour different sections of the walls via numerous promenades, while the Fossé Walks are placed beyond the walls and provide a sense of the structure.

The Basilique St-Sauveur, a Romanesque and Gothic edifice surrounded by exquisite gardens, is one of the most prominent churches in the old town. This cathedral houses the heart of Bertrand Du Guesclin, a 14th century fighter (the remainder of him is buried in St-Denis, near Paris).

The Tour de l'Horloge (Clock Tower) in the town centre provides spectacular views of Dinan and the Rance valley, but you must be willing to climb the 157 steps to get there. A note also warns that the bells will sound every hour and quarter hour, so be prepared!

Take a trip up the Rance, either by renting a motorboat and piloting it yourself, or by river launch to St-Malo, which is approximately 35 kilometres (22 miles) north.

Dinan is located 53 kilometres (33 miles) north of Rennes, the regional capital of Brittany, and 58 kilometres (36 miles) southeast of Mont St-Michel in nearby Normandy.

You'll feel as if you've gone back in time after a few days in Dinan. It's a pleasant place to roam around, learn about history, eat (crêpes and cider abound), and enjoy the surroundings.

The Office du Tourisme de Dinan is located just inside the city walls, between the massive parking lot at Place du Guesclin and the Château, which houses the Dinan Museum.

The Office can provide maps outlining self-guided walking tours of the city.

Dinan Tourism Bureau
9 rue du Château, BP 65 261
22105 DINAN Cedex
Tél: 02.96.876.976
Fax: 02.96.876.977

Hotels:

When traveling, it's advisable to book your hotel in advance. I recommend using Booking.com for great deals, and it is available for some hotels in any country. Scan the QR code to learn more. Here are some recommended hotels to consider

Hotel De La Porte in Saint Malo
- Location: 35 Rue Saint-Malo
- Phone: +33 2 96 39 19 76

This peaceful Saint Malo retreat provides relaxed lodgings with balconies, garden charm, and free Wi-Fi.

The Citi Hotel Le Challonge
- Location: 29 Pl. Duguesclin
- Phone: +33 2 96 87 16 30
Step back in time at this laid-back 1800s hotel, which features simplicity, a restaurant/bar, and the charm of Duguesclin Square.

Hotel Le Connetable
- Location: 8 Av. René Cassin.
- Phone: +33 2 96 87 29 29
This lively Dinan retreat features lively rooms, spa luxury with a hot tub, and the convenience of a kitchenette.

ibis Styles Dinan Centre-Ville
- Location: 1 Place Duclos Pinot
- Phone: +33 2 96 39 46 15
This simple Dinan Centre-Ville hotel offers modern accommodations, modest meals, beverages, and free Wi-Fi.

The Originals Boutique, Hôtel du Château, Dinan (Inter-Hotel)
- Location: 6 Rue du Château
- Phone: +33 2 96 85 16 20
This efficient boutique hotel in the centre of Dinan provides contemporary simplicity, a welcome bar and BMGcomplimentary Wi-Fi.

Leisure Activities:

Here are some more activities and excursions in the city or nearby to get involved in:

- Rent an Electric Boat in Rance

Outdoor Recreation: Exploring nature and the great outdoors

Saint-Samson-sur-Rance (5.3 km from Dinan)

Price range: 35-70 euros

Explore the Rance River's biodiversity and vegetation in electric boats, kayaks, and more, with walks lasting 1 to 3 hours.

- Saint-Malo Segway Tour

Recreational activity

Saint-Malo (22 km from Dinan).

Price range: 29-45 €

Gyromalo's fun Segway tours uncover hidden gems and Malouine history along sporty trails, allowing you to see Saint-Malo in a new perspective.

- Take a private cruise from Pointe du Grouin to Cap Fréhel.

Outdoor Recreation: Exploring nature and the great outdoors

The site is Saint-Malo.

Price range: €160 to €400

Up to 7 people can be accommodated for private sea walks along the Emerald Coast.

- A Vedette Boat travels from Dinard to Saint-Malo.

Outdoor Recreation: Exploring nature and the great outdoors

The locale is Dinard.

Price: 8 €

Festivals and Events:

Attending the events listed below in the city or nearby can make your trip memorable.

Take a regular line crossing from Saint-Malo to Dinard, Ile Cézembre or Iles Chausey to experience the grandeur of the North Brittany Coast.

Market on Thursday morning.
The Remparts Festival is held in July every two years.

Dinan Short Film Festival is a film festival that takes place in Dinan, Scotland.

End-of-August jazz festival for insiders and the curious on Place Saint-Sauveur.

Théâtre en Rance is a cultural organisation that hosts events in Dinan and the surrounding area:
The Théâtre en Rance festival, held every May, brings together and exchanges professional and amateur practises (theatre, music, and young audiences).

Les Jacobambins is the Young Audience season at the Théâtre des Jacobins.

RenC'arts is located beneath the Ramparts and hosts the Summer Street Arts Festival.
The early childhood event Premiers Émois.

Shopping:
While in the city, make sure to visit these recommended shops for a memorable shopping experience. You can bring back some souvenirs from your trip.

- Dinan Quevert Carrefour Commercial Centre
- Shopping mall

- Place: Quévert, France
- Phone: +33 826 25 32 35

- Dress Shop
- Store for Women's Clothing
- Address: Pass. The Tour de Force
- Phone: +33 6 64 62 41 94

- CB D'eau CBD Magasin DINAN
- Herb shop is a category.
- Address: 21 bis Pass. The Tour de Force
- Phone: +33 7 52 03 07 31

- AF NAF
- Store for Women's Clothing
- Address: 1 Place du, Rue du Marchix
- Phone: +33 2 96 85 02 05

- DistriCenter Dinan/Quevert Magasin
- Clothing store type
- Place: Quévert, France
- Phone: +33 2 96 39 42 55

- Dinan Lingerie Secret
- Lingerie store type
- Address: 50 Rue du Marchix
- Phone: +33 2 96 83 57 95

Restaurants:

For a relaxed and enjoyable dining experience, try any of the following top restaurants. I've included their contact details:

Le Cantorbery
- Location: 6 Rue Sainte-Claire
- Phone: +33 2 96 39 02 52
Le Cantorbery, a Brittany treasure, serves classics like Breton Galette in a welcoming atmosphere.

Restaurant Atypic
- Location: 14-16 Rue de la Poissonnerie, Paris, France
- Phone: +33 2 96 80 52 08
In a lively dine-in atmosphere, discover culinary innovation with Brittany delicacies like Far Breton at Restaurant Atypic.

Terre-Neuvas
- Location: 25 Rue du Quai
- Phone: +33 2 96 39 86 45
Cotriade is served in a traditional dine-in setting at Auberge des Terre-Neuvas, a taste of marine Brittany.

Le Resto
- Location: 7 Rue de la Ferronnerie
- Phone: +33 2 96 84 40 20
The stylish setting of Le Resto provides cosmopolitan dinners with a Brittany flair, such as Kouign-Amann, and it closes at 1:30 p.m.

La Lycorne

- Location: 6 Rue de la Poissonnerie
- Phone: +33 2 96 39 08 13

La Lycorne, a Brittany treasure, allows visitors to dine on regional specialties including Breton Crepes. There is no option for delivery.

Morlaix

Squeezed into a small valley created by the streams Le Queffleuth and Le Jarlot, which flow into the Rade de Morlaix, which connects to La Manche (the English Channel), is Morlaix, a key population centre in this region of Finistère with 15,000 residents.

Five centuries ago, the trade in linen was a major source of income for this region, and merchants who made their fortune on this trade built several streets of mediaeval half-timbered houses and granite mansions in Morlaix.

Transportation

Train Transportation Direct On the Paris-Brest route, TGV trains departing from Paris-Montparnasse take 3 to 3-1/2 hours to reach the Gare de Morlaix SNCF, located at Place du Colonel Rol Tanguy.

The Gare has two entrances, one on either side of the road. There are buses and shuttles available for the south side. There is a steep 62-meter (203-foot) step drop beneath the train bridge to the town centre, and the station is 15 minutes' walk away.

Public transit
Public transport in Morlaix and the surrounding area is operated by Lineotim. From the South (Sud) side of the Gare de Morlaix SNCF, the free Shuttle N2 takes nine minutes to get to the town centre (Place Cornic Trégor and Hôtel de Ville). The all-electric shuttles operate every 25 minutes starting at 7:00 a.m. Shuttles run from 7:00 a.m. to 7:00 p.m., Monday through Saturday (no shuttles on Sundays or holidays).

Bus
Buses 1 and 3 connect the town centre (Hôtel de Ville and Place Cornic Trégor) and the Gare (south side) every 30 minutes, approximately from 7:00 a.m. to 19:45 (7:45 p.m.). It takes 5 minutes to get from the train station to the centre. On the other hand, buses are not available on Sundays or holidays.

Tourist Office

Situated in the town centre at 10 Place Charles-de-Gaulle, the helpful Office de Tourisme (tel. +33 (0) 2 98 62 14 94, info@tourisme-morlaix.bzh) can be reached. Maps and leaflets detailing walking tours of Morlaix and driving excursions to other sites like the enclos paroissiaux, Carantec and other coastal sights are also included.

There are several different creperies and other casual dining options. Take a walk around some of the pedestrian streets, including rue Ange de Guernisac, as there isn't much to see on the main street. On that street, at La Crêpe Enchantée, we had a great many crêpes (and many glasses of wine). Near Place des Otages, at the Grand Café de la Terrasse, we also had some excellent moules frites.

Things to See

The viaduct, a massive structure that archefully spans the town, is the first object you see when you arrive in Morlaix. People can cross at the lower level, which offers fantastic views of Morlaix, even though trains pass over it. You'll need to climb numerous flights of steps to reach the bottom level, which is still rather high. The venelle de la Roche, or "alley of la Roche," is located on the west side of the major road, close to the Place des Otages, and offers better access. Once you've crossed, proceed along the venelle aux Prêtres, which will lead you past a number of private residences and eventually some quaint pedestrian streets like the rue Ange de Guernisac.

It has a number of restaurants and is bordered by historic homes.

Morlaix is home to a large number of exquisitely maintained houses from the 15th and 16th centuries, many of which are gathered around Place Allende and La Grand'Rue. The Maison de la Duchesse Anne, which dates back to 1530, is well-known for displaying a typical interior of the period.

Check out La Maison Pondalez at 9 Grand Rue as well. This 16th-century mansion's massive granite fireplace unites the various levels and architectural elements. Today, it serves as a museum where guests may view the ornate architecture typical of these historic residences. Because the middle of each of them featured an open courtyard, they were called "lantern houses".

The chambers also include antique secular and religious objects. The displays that focused on the production and trade of linen and flax, two businesses that brought significant affluence to this region in the 15th and 16th centuries, piqued our curiosity. The profits from the linen trade were used to construct the magnificent enclos paroissiaux, or parish closes, in this region. Large sums were expended in enclosures because every town insisted on having the nicest one. (Please remember that the exhibits related to the linen trade are borrowed from the Morlaix Museum and will probably be returned after restoration.)

Strolling along the shore or through the historic streets is calming. Don't miss the Saturday market in Place Allende if you're in town. There are lots of fresh vegetables, seafood, and other delectable foods available at this bustling market, along with apparel and home goods. Seek for the vendor who brings an entire roasted pig and keeps serving plates of meat until it's all gone, or the stand offering Kig Ha Farz, a Breton stew made with dumplings made of buckwheat and three different types of meat.

Morlaix excursions suggestions

As mentioned before, Morlaix makes an excellent starting point for exploring the surroundings. We took two excursions: one to the stunning enclos paroissiaux, which is only a short drive from Morlaix; the other was to the Neolithic burial mound known as the Cairn of Barnenez, which is located at Plouezoc'h on the Kernéléhen Peninsula, 14 kilometers/9 miles north of Morlaix.

From Morlaix, it is simple to travel to Roscoff, Carantec, and Saint-Pol-de-Léon.

Hotels:

When traveling, it's advisable to book your hotel in advance. I recommend using Booking.com for great deals, and it is available for some hotels in any country. Scan the QR code to learn more. Here are some recommended hotels to consider

- The Port Hotel - 3 Quai de Léon - Tel: +33 2 98 88 07 54

The combination of a modern 19th-century residence, minimalist bar, free Wi-Fi, and spectacular river views makes for an amazing stay.

- Hotel De L'Europe - 1 Rue d'Aiguillon - Tel: +33 2 98 62 11 99

A nice, friendly atmosphere is created by the easygoing charm, magnificent lounge bar and elegant breakfast room.

- Hotel Saint-Melaine - 75 Rue Ange de Guernisac - +33 2 98 88 54 76

Colourful, uncomplicated rooms in a relaxed location, with a restaurant and a lively bar for an unforgettable experience.

- L'Albatros - Imp. De Coat, Menguy - Phone: +33 2 98 88 08 44

This hotel is simple, with a modern restaurant and spa, including an indoor pool, for a pleasant and relaxing stay.

- Hotel Fontaine Logis - 7 Rue Jean François Periou - +33 2 98 62 09 55

With free WiFi, a bar, restaurant, and bike storage, this hotel provides a comfortable and convenient stay.

- Duc de Bretagne Luxury Appart'hotel - 3 Rpe Saint-Melaine - Phone: +33 6 95 59 33 99

Luxury apartments in Saint-Melaine offer an exclusive and upmarket experience in the centre of the city.

Festivals and Events:
Attending the events listed below in the city or nearby can make your trip memorable.

Panoramas is a three-day festival in early April that features concerts and shows in electro music, rock, hip-hop, cine-concerts, dance, and theatre.

Every Wednesday of the beautiful season, from July 14th until mid-August, Le Bel Été, which premiered during the June music festival, hosts concerts or street shows. On the second Sunday of July, there is also a Breton festival. The event is completely free to attend.

The Ronde du Viaduc bicycle race draws a significant crowd in July, while the semi-marathon Saint-Pol of Léon-Morlaix on the first weekend of November brings the city to life.

Finally, Place des Otages, Place Souvestre, and Place Allende exhibit seafood and the unique Breton terroir during the weekly market on Saturday.

Leisure Activities:
Here are some more activities and excursions in the city or nearby to get involved in:

Roscoff Exotic Botanical Garden - €3-€6 per person.
Discover "The Southern Hemisphere in Northern Finistere" on 16,000 m2 in Roscoff's botanical sanctuary, 18.6 km from Morlaix.

Musical Tour of The Sound of Music in Rustic Brittany - €17
An outdoor musical trip from Morlaix takes you 41 kilometres via Meneham, Pays Pagan, and North Finistère.

Shopping:
While in the city, make sure to visit these recommended shops for a memorable shopping experience. You can bring back some souvenirs from your trip.

Le Galerie - Shopping Mall - Saint Martin des Champs, France - Phone: +33 2 98 63 94 00

La Galerie, Saint Martin des Champs' popular shopping core, is open until 7:30 p.m. for in-store purchases and pick-up.

MagasinDistriCenter-Morlaix/Saint-Martin-Des-Champs - Clothing Store Category - CENTRE COMMERCIAL - Phone: +33 2 98 63 47 51 Magasin DistriCenter in Morlaix/Saint-Martin-Des-Champs sells trendy products. Shop in-store or choose easy pick-up options till 7 p.m.

Casino Drive Morlaix - Shopping Mall - St-Martin-des-Champs, France - Phone: +33 2 98 63 94 00
Casino Drive Morlaix, a Saint-Martin-des-Champs shopping zone, offers in-store pick-up and delivery until 8 p.m.

BIBBY MORLAIX - Clothing Store Category - Saint-Martin-des-Champs, France Hometown
BIZZBEE in Morlaix sells trendy apparel. Shop in-store or select easy pick-up options till 7:30 p.m.

Morlaix Black Market - Clothing Store Category - Saint-Martin-des-Champs, France - Phone: +33 2 21 62 00 65
Morlaix's Black Store is open for business until 7pm

Micromania by Zing MORLAIX - Video Game Store - Location: Geant Commercial MORLAIX Saint Martin des Champs - Phone: +33 2 56 45 01 59

Micromania - Zing MORLAIX is a gaming arcade located in Geant MORLAIX Saint Martin des Champs Centre Commercial. Purchase in-store or pick-up in-store till 7:30 p.m.

Restaurants:
For a relaxed and enjoyable dining experience, try any of the following top restaurants. I've included their contact details:

Crêperie de l'Océan - 2 Rue de la Villeneuve - Tél: +33 2 98 15 24 02
Crêperie l'Océane, which serves savoury galettes and offers the best of Brittany, is open when others are closed.

The Grand Café at The Terrace - 31 Pl. des Otages - +33 2 98 88 20 25
Le Grand Café de la Terrasse provides dine-in elegance with regional cuisine rather than takeaway.

CASA VECCHIA - 13 Rue Ange de Guernisac - Tel: +33 2 98 88 18 90
With takeaway options, pasta, and regional pleasures, CASA VECCHIA offers an Italian flair.

La Boucherie in Coat Menguy - Phone: +33 2 98 88 08 78
The chophouse La Boucherie, which serves the finest Brittany meats, shuts at 2 p.m.

L'Hermine - 35 Rue Ange de Guernisac - Tel: +33 2 98 88 10 91
L'Hermine provides delectable Brittany crêpes in a nice setting till 2 p.m.

Atipik Bilig - 1 Rue Ange de Guernisac - Tel: +33 2 98 62 47 62
Atipik Bilig is a one-of-a-kind crêperie that shuts at 2 p.m. and specialises in unique buckwheat cuisine.

Paimpont and Brocéliande Forest

In addition to its Celtic roots, Brittany is well-known for its enigmatic past. The standing stones of Carnac, the Quiberon Peninsula, the quaint hamlet of Josselin, the small village of Vannes, and other attractions may be found in the central region of Brittany, which is primarily in the Morbihan department.

The Paimpont Forest, in the heart of Brocéliande, is the setting for many of the Merlin legends. A large portion of the Morbihan is covered with forests. The legend states that Merlin moved to the Forest of Brocéliande to dwell alone. Nevertheless, he instead encountered and became enamoured with the fairy Viviane. He was trapped in a magic circle by her using her skills, and he remained there.

With Restaurants and stores bearing the names of Viviane, Merlin, and other characters, Paimpont, the principal town of Brocéliande, takes its reputation as the epicentre of Merlin lore very seriously. The Tourist Information Office is located at the far end of the town's main street, which is lined with a variety of stores and eateries.

You can get information about several walking trails and a map of the area from the Office. These include the Merlin Walk, which leads to the Fountain of Youth and Merlin's mausoleum; the Valley of No Return circuit; and a romantic stroll around the little lake in the middle of Paimpont.

The address of the Paimpont, France tourist information centre is 1 Pl. du Roi Saint-Judicael, 35380 Paimpont, France. The phone number is +33 2 99 07 84 23.

We chose to go to Merlin's grave. Both the tomb and the walk from the parking lot to it were rather easy. We decided to carry on walking and soon came across the Fountain of Youth (I'm not sure if it works, though...) and a little pond. Nevertheless, there was very little signage for the walk once we left the tomb and the fountain, and some of the paths were difficult to find. It was okay that we eventually went back the same way we had arrived. Maybe the indicators will get better, but don't expect much help. Perhaps magic was meant to be used by mankind

Brittany Merlin's Tomb... Merlin's Tomb. It's meant to be covered in holly, but we couldn't find any.

We had two enjoyable breaks on the way from Brest to Paimpont. We started by going back to Josselin, which we had adored visiting a few years prior. We enjoyed lunch in the plaza near the lovely church, strolled through the heart of this old town, and marvelled at the château. Josselin, which dates back to the eleventh century, boasts intriguing architecture in addition to a lengthy and well-preserved history.

We also deviated from the path when we came across a sign for the Château de Trécesson. We had no prior knowledge of it, but after a short drive down a winding dirt road, there it was, exquisitely reflected in the pond that surrounded it. We only got to see it from the outside because it is only open to guests in July and August. A delightful little diversion!

Only 11 kilometres (7 miles) separate Château de Trecesson in Brittany from Paimpont.

Paimpont doesn't have many lodging options, but the surrounding towns and countryside do. You are able to look at this. A modest B&B in the country welcomed us with the sounds of birds, ducks, and frogs.

Regarding Merlin? He failed to make an appearance.

Restaurants:

For a relaxed and enjoyable dining experience, try any of the following top restaurants. I've included their contact details:

- Le Pont du Secret - Phone: +33 2 56 49 60 61 - Location: Le Pont du Secret
  - Specialties: Traditional Breton food, including the savoury Galette Bretonne and sweet Far Breton.

- L'Atelier - Phone: +33 2 23 43 31 50 - Address: 25 Esp. de Brocéliande
  - Highlights: Culinary craftsmanship with a regional flair, with delicacies such as Kouign-Amann and Cider-Infused Pork.

- Les Forges de Paimpont Restaurant - Plélan-le-Grand, France - Phone: +33 2 99 06 81 07
  - Specifications: Enjoy authentic Breton cuisine such as Bouillabaisse and Crepes with Salted Caramel.

- Brocéliande Pas Sage
- Address: 2 Rue des Forges - Téléphone: +33 6 45 41 59 88

Casual appeal, presenting traditional Breton sandwiches such as Jambon-Beurre and Andouille.

- Crêperie La Fée Gourmande - Address: 16 Av. du Chevalier Ponthus - Phone: +33 2 99 07 89 63 - Specialties: Sweet and savoury crêpes, including Crêpe Complète and Salted Caramel Crêpe.

- Terrasse de l'abbaye - 2 Av. du Chevalier Ponthus - Phone: +33 2 99 07 81 12

- Highlights include scenic dining with Breton treats such as Cotriade and Kouign-Amann for a true sense of Brittany.

Leisure Activities:
Here are some more activities and excursions in the city or nearby to get involved in:

On-Foot Observation (6 €): Walk around the 25-hectare wildlife park of La Ferme du Monde and see 400 semi-free roaming animals from 5 continents. 24 kilometres away from Paimpont.

PDAL Kart Adventure (9 €): Take a fast-paced PEDAL kart ride across the park's various environments and get up close and personal with nature. 24 kilometres away from Paimpont.

Festivals and Events:
Attending the events listed below in the city or nearby can make your trip memorable.

- Don't miss Brocéliande's Rencontres de l'Imaginaire in July. A week full of events, conferences, and performances is planned for both young and old.

- Come to the Paimpont Forest Art and Nature Festival on a weekend in mid-September. There are suggested films, cartoons, seminars, and exhibitions centred around the theme of nature for a memorable weekend.

- Three days of street entertainment are scheduled for Paimpont as part of the Festival Stop Your Circus at the beginning of June. a significant and important occasion in the town, which for a few days is pulsated by circus acts.

Shopping:
While in the city, make sure to visit these recommended shops for a memorable shopping experience. You can bring back some souvenirs from your trip.

Broceliande Art et Artisanat - Type: Gift Shop - Address: 18 Rue du Général de Gaulle

Les Trésors de Brocéliande - Address: 2 Rue du Général de Gaulle - Phone: +33 6 10 47 55 98 - Type: Gift Shop

La Maison du Graal - Address: 21 bis Rue du Général de Gaulle - Phone: +33 2 99 07 83 82 - Type: Gift Basket Store

Arcanes et Secrets - Category: Store - Location: 16 Rue du Général de Gaulle - Phone: +33 6 31 06 39 05

Fleurs de Peau - Category: Clothing Store - Location: Les Rues Coudées - Phone: +33 6 49 60 45 03

Au Pays de Merlin - Gift Basket Store - 28 Rue du Général de Gaulle - Phone: +33 2 99 07 80 2

crêpes

Perros-Guirec

Perros-Guirec, located at the extremity of a peninsula in Brittany's Côtes-d'Armor Département, promotes "la vie en roz." The pink granite coast line is indeed striking and gorgeous, and this charming ancient town is an excellent starting point for exploring it. It is located approximately 165 kilometres (just over 100 miles) northwest of St. Malo.

The town itself is small, with a year-round population of less than 10,000 people. Many visitors come to enjoy the beaches, while others come to walk the Custom Officers' Path, a picturesque trail along the red cliffs. The town has several restaurants, shops, and grocery stores, as well as various locations to buy beach attire and toys, and, of course, ice cream!

Perros-Guirec Sentier des Douaniers
There are so many lovely rock formations along the
Sentier des Douaniers!

What to see
Perros-Guirec is a fantastic area to spend time outside! The highlights are the beaches and the Sentier des Douaniers (a walking track along the red granite shore).

If you enjoy beaches, there are numerous to pick from. The Plage de Trestraou is the largest and closest to the town centre. This 1.4-kilometer-long beach is fairly broad during low tide and provides ample space for swimming and sunbathing. There are a variety of eateries along the waterfront, as well as changing rooms and bathrooms.
Trestraou is also the departure point for excursion boats. One of the most popular trips is to the Seven Islands, an archipelago with notable bird sanctuaries, including a nesting site for the famous "fou de bassan," or gannets. You should book the boat ahead of time because they do fill up.

The Plage de Trestrignel is a second beach near the peninsula's tip. Aside from the beach, it provides beautiful views of some of the area's houses.

Plage de Saint-Guirec, the third beach, is significantly smaller but equally beautiful. Saint-Guirec was a Welsh monk who moved to Brittany in the sixth century to establish a monastery. On this beach, the 11th-century Oratory of Saint-Guirec (restored in 2021) stands, with a chapel behind it. Women have come for decades to pray for their husbands who were at sea or to find a husband. The current stone monument dates from 1904; the original wood statue is housed in the chapel.

I arrived at the Oratory after walking around Le Sentier des Douaniers, one of the most enjoyable activities in Perros-Guirec. The Sentier, which was built in 1791 and used by customs officers to combat smuggling, is one of Brittany's most famous hiking trails, running 2000 kilometres along the coast from Mont-Saint-Michel to Saint-Nazaire. You may pick up the Côte Rose section of the path in Perros-Guirec and have a delightful walk among the magnificent pink granite.

The colours of the rocks got more vibrant as the fog crept in.
You may either walk from the Plage de Trestraou or drive a little further and park at Le Ranolien. We walked along the coast from there, taking in the sights (including the Men Ruz lighthouse, which was visible in the fog both times we passed by). We made a pit break at

the Maison du littoral, a welcome centre where you can purchase a tiny brochure identifying the landmarks along the route.

I continued on to the port of Ploumanac'h, which has been a fishing centre since Gallo-Roman times, after a picnic in Saint-Guirec. Despite the fact that it is largely utilised for pleasure craft these days, there are still a few fishing boats, as well as restaurants and picnic sites.

Brittany's Ploumanac'h
A couple of boats in Ploumanac'h harbour.
You'll also witness a few buildings or the remains of buildings along the way, some of which date from more recent times. The Men Ruz lighthouse, for example, was destroyed on August 4, 1944, and rebuilt in 1947 from pink granite.

A stroll down the Sentier des Douaniers is a pleasant way to spend a few hours (we recommend going in the morning because it is less crowded than in the afternoon). The path is largely wide and level, with some opportunity to climb over boulders. Saint-Guirec boasts a number of restaurants, boulangeries, and ice cream stores, and it's a fantastic place to stop on the route.

Information for Tourists
The Tourist Information Office is located at 21, Place de l'Hôtel de Ville (+33 (0)2 96 23 21 15) and may be identified by its pink "La Vie en Roz" banners. They include maps of the area as well as information about

the beaches and the Sentier des Douaniers. While you're there, check out the beautiful Hôtel de Ville across the street.

Hotels
Perros-Guirec is well-known for its charming little hotels, many of which are housed in old structures. Les Hydrangéas, a tiny and freshly rebuilt hotel near the Plage de Trestrignel, provided me with a pleasant stay.
Perros Guirec Hydrangeas
View from our balcony.

Perros-Guirec Fun Fact: In The Phantom of the Opera, Christine's scarf is blown into the sea and saved by Raoul de Chagny many years before they meet at the opera. It is also the location of Christine's father's burial and the location where the Phantom plays her father's violin for her.

We took a gorgeous drive along the coast from Perros-Guirec, including a lovely side detour for a picnic on l'Île Grande, a little island reachable by a bridge right after the village of Penvern. I drove for a bit, not knowing where I was heading, hoping to locate a suitable area to stop, and voilà! A charming small fishing spot with tables and a hiking track. My favourite part was the aluminium fish table with the statement (in French) "Hello, next sale Thursday June 15, 10:30-18:00, fish and shellfish, according to arrival." I wish I could have stayed for some of that delicious fresh seafood!

Instead, I continued on to the intriguing Cairn of Barnenez, a Neolithic tomb dating back to 4500 BCE. It is well worth a visit. From there, I travelled to Morlaix, which is an excellent base for exploring the Enclos Paroissiaux.

When traveling, it's advisable to book your hotel in advance. I recommend using Booking.com for great deals, and it is available for some hotels in any country. Scan the QR code to learn more. Here are some recommended hotels to consider

- Best Western Hotel Perros Guirec - Hotel & Spa Les Bains - 100 Avenue du Casino - Phone: +33 2 96 91 22 11

Unfussy hotel with a bar, sauna spa and free Wi-Fi that provides a pleasant stay on the shore.

- Ploumanac'h Perros-Guirec Hôtel de l'Europe - Location: PLOUMANACH - 158 Rue Saint-Guirec - Phone: +33 2 96 91 40 76

Casual rooms with balconies at a calm hotel with sea views and free Wi-Fi for a peaceful stay.

- Hôtel view mer Perros-Guirec le Nautica - 87 Rue Ernest Renan - Phone: +33 2 96 14 20 68

Rooms with bay views in a casual hotel with a lounge, providing a cosy coastal hideaway.

- Citotel Les Sternes – Rte de Perros – Phone: +33 2 96 91 03 38

In a basic hotel with a breakfast choice and a terrace, there are casual rooms, some with sea views.

- Villa les Hydrangeas - Hôtel restaurant view mer - Address: 53 Boulevard Georges Clémenceau - Phone: +33 2 96 23 22 94

Rooms with sea views that are informal and simple, with free parking and Wi-Fi for a relaxing beach stay.

Leisure Activities:

Here are some more activities and excursions in the city or nearby to get involved in:

- Roscoff Exotic Botanical Garden: - Prices range from 3 € to 6 €.

Discover the "Southern Hemisphere in Northern Finistere" in this 16000 m2 garden located 40 kilometres from Perros-Guirec.

Festivals and Events:

Attending the events listed below in the city or nearby can make your trip memorable.

Friday morning market in the city centre.

Gastronomy salon (Easter).

Spring comic book festival (April).

In August, there is a Hydrangea Festival.

On Tuesdays (July-August Trestraou), there will be a craft market and a performance.

Ploumanac'h old rigs, nighttime concerts, and fireworks on holidays.

In the bay, feast on Venetian harbour. Late July, 20 kilometres from the Côte de Granit Rose.

Shopping:
While in the city, make sure to visit these recommended shops for a memorable shopping experience. You can bring back some souvenirs from your trip.

GALLERIES KER Iliz - Type: Gift Shop - Address: 6 Rue du Général de Gaulle - Shopping: In-store - Contact: +33 2 96 91 00 96

Le Comptoir de Ploumanac'h - Type: Gift Shop - Address: 157 Rue Saint-Guirec - Shopping: In-store - Contact: +33 2 96 91 46 18

Un Point C'est Tout - Store - Address: 2 Rue du Général de Gaulle - Shopping: In-store shopping - Phone: +33 2 96 37 72 06

Galeries Saint Guirec - Type: Clothing Store - Address: Rue Saint-Guirec - Shopping: In-Store

Aux trois mousquetons
   - Type: Clothing Store - Address: 91 Rue Ernest Renan
- Shopping: In-store - Phone: +33 2 96 46 30 42

La Craquanterie - Type: Gift Basket Store - Address: 4
Rue Ernest Renan - Shopping: In-store - Phone: +33 2
96 46 33 70

Restaurants:
For a relaxed and enjoyable dining experience, try any of
the following top restaurants.

Mor's Coste
   - Address: 162 Rue Saint-Guirec, 22700 Perros-Guirec
- Phone number: +33 2 96 91 65 55
   - Specifications: A seafood lover's paradise on the
coast. Try the Bouillabaisse and relax in a nautical
setting.

Le Ker Bleu Restaurant - Pg Trestraou, 17 Bd Joseph le
Bihan - Phone: +33 2 96 91 14 69 Beachfront pleasure
providing delectable Pizza Provençale and daily catch.

Restaurant l'Ardoise - 80 Rue Ernest Renan - Phone:
+33 2 96 23 22 88 - Specialties: A lively brasserie that
serves Tarte Flambée and superb seafood dishes.

La Crémaillère - 13 Place de l'Église - Phone: +33 2 96
23 22 08 Traditional seafood destination. Bouedec, a

classic Breton fisherman's stew, and other dishes are available.

Quiberon

The Quiberon Peninsula, also known as the Presqu'île de Quiberon, is a stunning little peninsula in southern Brittany that is only a few miles (10 kilometres) long on each end. It is located south of Carnac.

Quiberon Peninsula

Quiberon provides visitors with a great deal of variety. It is well-known for its sandy beaches on Quiberon Bay and its Côte Sauvage, or Wild Coast, on the Atlantic side. There are numerous hiking trails throughout the mountains, and more roads lead to the sea. Many minor settlements have grown, but the main tourist destinations are the towns of Quiberon, which is located closer to the southern tip of the peninsula, and St-Pierre-Quiberon, which is located further north.

Beautiful strolling routes and expansive views may be found at the Pointe du Conguel, the peninsula's southernmost point. If you visit during exceptionally low tides, like we did, you will witness a large number of people fishing for prawns, mussels, periwinkles and other shellfish using nets and baskets. When you're there, have dinner with seafood!

Ferries depart at Quiberon's pier if you're going to one of the coastal islands, like Belle-Île, Houat, or Hoëdic.

Tourist Information Quiberon, France 14 Rue de Verdun, 56174 Quiberon, +33 (0) 825 135600

Hotels:

When traveling, it's advisable to book your hotel in advance. I recommend using Booking.com for great deals, and it is available for some hotels in any country. Scan the QR code to learn more. Here are some recommended hotels to consider

Best Western Hôtel Le Bellevue - 4 Rue du Tiviec - Tel: +33 2 97 50 16 28

A modern hotel with discreet rooms, some with views of the ocean, and an outdoor pool for a pleasant visit.

Albatros - 19 Rue de Port Maria - Telephone: +33 2 97 50 15 05

Airy, simple rooms in a laid-back hotel with a seafood restaurant and magnificent sea views.

Hôtel des Druides – 6 Rue de Port Maria – Phone: +33 2 97 50 14 74

Simple rooms with balconies and bay views, free Wi-Fi, and a seafood restaurant ensure a relaxing stay.

Hôtel de la Mer - Phone: +33 2 97 50 09 05 - Address: 8 Quai de Houat

Simple rooms in a laid-back hotel with an indoor/outdoor pool, bar and seafood restaurant.

Hôtel La Petite Sirène - Address: 15 Boulevard René Cassin - Phone: +33 2 97 50 17 34

A bayside hotel with light, uncomplicated rooms and suites, an optional breakfast buffet and a friendly bar.

Leisure Activities:
Here are some more activities and excursions in the city or nearby to get involved in:

Outdoor Show: Eternal Sarah Bernhardt - Activity: Sauzon Entertainment - Price: 14 Euro

Explore Sarah Bernhardt's island refuge with an outdoor show on Belle-Île-en-Mer, 14.5 miles from Quiberon.

Drawing/Painting/3D Art Classes in Erdeven - Activity: Arts and Crafts - Price: 15 €

Participate in creative workshops at Erdeven, 17.9 kilometres from Quiberon, that promote artistic expression in a restored environment.

Cruise around the Gulf of Morbihan and the islands - Activity: Nature and the great outdoors in Vannes - Price: 25 €

Navix will take you on a South Brittany tour, exploring the Gulf of Morbihan and adjacent islands for marine delights.

Stroll on an Old Rigging on the Gulf of Morbihan - Activity: Nature and the great outdoors in Arradon - Price: 40 € to 80 €

Sail on the Lys Noir, a historic French ship near Arradon, 26 kilometres from Quiberon, for an unforgettable adventure in the Gulf of Morbihan.

Fun Food-Themed Trail in the World of Carabreizh - Activity: Landévant Entertainment - Price: 0 € to 3 €

Discover caramel and fruity sweets on a wonderful walk at Le Monde de Carabreizh in Landévant, 31 kilometres from Quiberon.

Festivals and Events:
Attending the events listed below in the city or nearby can make your trip memorable.

Quiberon Fest is an April celebration of fun activities and entertainment. All are welcome to sign up and take advantage of the following events and activities: guided walks, nature walks, kid-friendly library workshops, outdoor games and inflatables, boat trips, diving, yachting, kayaking, swimming, riding, golf, tennis, sea fishing, and flying trips.

Summer concert series: Quiberon hums with music from many genres: Fest Noz, music, concerts, customary celebrations: Saint-Jacques shell festival of the sardines.
September: rally moped disguised as a triathlon.
A Breton artist's concert in October as part of the "An Autumn That" event.

December: Quiberon hosts a Christmas market, an ice rink, and a variety of family-friendly events to celebrate the holiday.

Shopping:

While in the city, make sure to visit these recommended shops for a memorable shopping experience. You can bring back some souvenirs from your trip.

- Comptoir de la Mer Quiberon - Address: 3 Quai de l'Océan - Phone: +33 2 97 50 16 28 - Type: Clothing Store

Discover maritime clothes at Comptoir de la Mer in Quiberon, which offers a variety of trendy clothing for ocean lovers.

- La Boutique de Pont Aven - Category: Convenience Store - Location: 16 Pl. Hoche - Phone: +33 2 97 50 18 26

Visit La Boutique de Pont Aven in Quiberon for a convenient shopping experience that offers necessities in the centre of the town.

- Un Été La Mer - Category: Clothing Store - Location: Pl. Hoche - Phone: +33 2 97 30 46 87

Dive into summer style at Un Été La Mer in Quiberon, which offers a seasonal clothing line.

- The British Cashmere - Address: 14 Rue de la Gare - Phone: +33 6 63 89 52 52 - Type: Clothing Store

The British Cashmere in Quiberon offers luxury and warmth with high-quality cashmere clothes.

- Les Pétroleuses - Address: 11 Pl. Hoche - Phone: +33 9 53 55 71 61 - Type: Women's Clothing Store

Les Pétroleuses in Quiberon offers sophisticated women's wear with a beautiful collection for every occasion.

- Saint James | Quiberon - Address: 2 Pl. Hoche - Phone: +33 2 97 12 39 37 - Type: Clothing Store

Saint James in Quiberon, noted for its quality apparel and marine flair, offers timeless and traditional styles.

Restaurants:

For a relaxed and enjoyable dining experience, try any of the following top restaurants. I've included their contact details:

Chez Diego - Boulevard de la Plage - Telephone: +33 2 97 50 19 99

Chez Diego serves French meals such as savoury crêpes and seafood delights, as well as Brittany cuisine.

Le Corsaire - Phone: +33 2 97 50 42 69 - Address: 24 Quai de Belle Île

Le Corsaire, famed for its seafood entrée and coastal appeal, serves French cooking by the sea.

Bistrot Gourmand La Mer à Boire

- Address: 1 Bd d'Hoedic - Telephone: +33 2 97 88 95 19

La Mer à Boire is a delightful café that serves excellent French meals with a gourmet twist.

Cap Au Large - Rue Port Maria, Promenade de la Plage - Phone: +33 2 97 30 39 93

Cap Au Large, a crêperie with Brittany classics and ocean views, has a coastal vibe.

Les Mouettes - Phone: +33 2 97 50 07 88 - Location: 10 Rte du Vivier

Les Mouettes serves French cuisine with a focus on Brittany dishes and a friendly atmosphere by the sea.

Quimper

Quimper is renowned globally for its unique faïence, which consists of hand-painted ceramic pieces that portray traditional Breton characters and scenes. Pottery has been produced in the Quimper region for more than three centuries.

In addition, it serves as the cultural hub of the historical Cornouaille region of Cornwall and the capital of the Finistère (Land's End) Department. Numerous names and signage can be found in Breton, such as Kemper, the town's name, and Ti and Douristed, the tourist office.

The town centre is bisected by the Odet River and a quaint little canal; boat tours on the Odet are available during certain seasons. The main attractions are easily accessible on foot in the old town centre, which boasts a sizable pedestrian zone.

The central plaza is dominated by the Cathédrale St-Corentin. Numerous cafés are available where you can have a meal or a drink while observing people. This enormous church dates from the 13th to the 19th century and is named for Saint Corentin, a Cornouaille bishop who lived in the fifth century. Beautiful stained glass and sculptures can be found within.

The Musée des Beaux-Arts, or Fine Arts Museum, is located just across the square from the Cathedral. It is mostly dedicated to European painting and features pieces by Quimper-born artist Max Jacob.

René Laennec, the man who invented the stethoscope, is another beloved son who has a statue in the main square!
A sizable museum in Quimper honours Breton heritage and history. The Cathedral is also close to the Musée Départemental Breton.

In addition to having lots of crêperies, Quimper is a hub of traditional Breton life. A great local dinner is made with cider and croissants. The aptly called Place au Beurre, or Butter Square, is surrounded by a number of eateries.

Located in the centre of the old town, on Rue Kéréon, is the primary shopping street. There are a variety of souvenirs and china available for purchase. The Halles, or food markets, are close by and are always a busy place to be.
You'll need to travel around 1.7 kilometres (one mile) southwest along the river to see more ceramics. The little Musée de la Faïence is located here; it is open seasonally; check with the Tourist Office. One of the most well-known factories, HB Henriot's, is also open for visits (contact for times and details).

Quimper is a historic city with remnants of its walls and towers still standing. The different sections of the walls are explained by signs in both Breton and French.

A trip to Quimper offers an insight into Breton customs, language, and culture. Quimper is a real working city and a pleasure to visit, despite being a little more remote and less touristy than some other sections of Brittany. The mediaeval villages of Josselin and Vannes, the Quiberon Peninsula, and Carnac, the location of ancient standing stones, are all only a short drive away.
Situated on the southern bank of the Odet River, directly beyond the Pont Max Jacob, lies the Quimper Tourist Information Office. Walking time from the main square by the Cathedral is around 6 to 8 minutes. Taking in the charming vistas of the town and river is a bonus for visiting.

Tourist Office
Place de la Résistance 29000 Quimper, +33 (0)2 98
5304 05

Hotels:
When traveling, it's advisable to book your hotel in advance. I recommend using Booking.com for great deals, and it is available for some hotels in any country. Scan the QR code to learn more. Here are some recommended hotels to consider

Hôtel Oceania Quimper – 17 Rue du Poher – Phone: +33 2 98 90 46 26

For a peaceful stay, this modern hotel features a casual restaurant, bar and a seasonal outdoor pool.

Hôtel Escale Oceania Quimper - 6 Rue Théodore le Hars - Tel: +33 2 98 53 37 37
For a cosy ambiance, this modern hotel has warmly designed rooms, a lobby bar and daily eating.

Best Western Plus Hôtel Kregenn - 13 Rue des Réguaires - Tel: +33 2 98 95 08 70
A beautiful getaway with Wi-Fi, breakfast, a trendy lounge bar and a walled garden.

Hôtel Mercure Quimper Centre - Phone: +33 2 98 90 31 71 - Address: 21 Bis Av. de la Gare
Relaxed hotel with a rooftop patio, bar, conference area and free Wi-Fi for a pleasant stay.

Brit Hotel Quimper Sud - 3 Avenue Georges Pompidou - Phone: +33 2 98 53 34 44
A simple yet inviting budget motel with unassuming rooms, garden access and an informal restaurant/bar.

Festivals and Events:
Attending the events listed below in the city or nearby can make your trip memorable.

Cornwall Festival Quimper, a spectacular rendezvous of Breton culture, attracts over 250,000 tourists every year for six days beginning on the third Sunday of July.

The Musical Weeks, which take place during the first three weeks of August, feature a dozen high-quality classical concerts.

From October to June Thursdays of the Bishopric, dance and traditional Breton music are performed in the Bishop's gardens every Thursday at 21h from mid-June to mid-September.

The festival "Theatre At Any Age" welcomes children and adults to a celebration in the streets and friendly rooms of Quimper in December before Christmas.

The rendezvous season, Event Circus, Cirque de Noel.
New School Hip Hop Festival, an October hip hop festival

Restaurants:
For a relaxed and enjoyable dining experience, try any of the following top restaurants. I've included their contact details:

- Buffalo Grill Quimper - All. Louis Jouvet ZAC de - Phone: +33 2 98 53 30 00

Steakhouse serving substantial Brittany gastronomy, including grilled meats and savoury crepes.

- Chez Claudius – 3 Bis Rue Jean Jaurès – Phone: +33 2 98 56 79 34

Classic bistro with a Brittany twist, providing hearty dishes like coq au vin and seafood.

- Le Bistrot de Louis - 101B Avenue de la France libre - Phone: +33 2 98 95 56 08

In a cosy atmosphere, a French café evoking the flavour of Brittany serves galettes, cider, and regional delights.

- KERMAM - Rue Gustave Eiffel, Quartier De L'Hippodrome

Local restaurant serving Brittany-inspired cuisine, including buckwheat pancakes and seafood specialties.

- Crêperie du Quartier - Address: 16 Rue du Sallé - Phone: +33 2 98 64 29 30

Charming creperie with a Brittany flair, serving sweet and savoury crepes with a selection of local ciders.

- Le Maharaja – 43 Bd Amiral de Kerguélen – Phone: +33 2 98 64 81 74

Authentic Indian cuisine with a Brittany twist, with curry dishes and aromatic spices served in a lively setting.

Shopping:
While in the city, make sure to visit these recommended shops for a memorable shopping experience. You can bring back some souvenirs from your trip.

- Commercial centre Carrefour Quimper - Shopping Mall - Location: 11 Rue du Poher - Phone: +33 2 98 98 08 79

A lively retail district with a wide range of stores, from fashion to electronics, as well as quick in-store purchasing and pick-up alternatives.

- Le Passage du Chapeau Rouge - Type: Shopping Mall - Address: 34 Rue du Chapeau Rouge Quaint shopping destination with a chosen mix of stores for an in-store shopping experience that is both unique and unhurried.

- Géant Quimper Gallery - Type: Shopping Mall - Address: 163 Rte de Bénodet - Phone: +33 2 98 10 04 00

Extensive retail complex with a diverse selection of stores ranging from fashion to electronics, as well as in-store shopping and pick-up services.

- LDL - Shopping Mall - Address: 37 Av. de la Liberté - Phone: +33 800 90 03 43

Local shopping location with a variety of stores and in-store shopping for a convenient retail experience.

- Quimper faience - Type: Outlet Store - Location: Pl. Denis Berardier - Phone: +33 2 98 90 09 36

Outlet store specialising in Quimper faience, with in-store shopping, pick-up, and delivery options for one-of-a-kind pottery finds.

Josselin

Josselin, with fewer than 3000 inhabitants, is a quiet town with a long history. Its famous château has been razed and rebuilt several times. Since the 15th century it has been owned by the Rohan family, who still reside there.

Guided tours are offered in season, allowing the visitor to see the interior of the château as well as its ornate inner façade, which is in sharp contrast to the fortress-like view from the river, the view presented to enemies. Carvings of animals and other designs, as well as stylized letters for the Rohan motto A Plus, make for an interesting façade.

Nearby is the Musée des Poupées, or Doll Museum, with over 500 dolls from the Rohan collection. A combined ticket with the château offers a discounted fee.
In the center of the village is the beautiful church, Basilique Notre-Dame-du-Roncier, or Our Lady of the Brambles. Legend has it that a farmer found a statue of the Virgen in a bramble bush on this spot in 808. It became a site of pilgrimage, and the legend further says that the farmer's daughter was cured of her blindness.

The church is Gothic, with wonderful gargoyles. It contains the tombs of Eudon 1er de Porhoet, the son of Josselin, and his wife, Anne de Leon, which date from the 11th century.
It is also possible to climb the Tower, for beautiful views of the Château de Josselin and the surrounding countryside.

A bit of history
Josselin's centre is a reflection of its lengthy past. Dedicated to his son, the mediaeval city was founded in the eleventh century by Guéthenoc, the Viscount of Porhoët, and has several lovely half-timbered homes still standing. A quick stroll around the area will pass many of these. Because of its skilled craftspeople, the town experienced enormous wealth in the seventeenth century. Additionally, the town saw an increase in trade

when the Nantes-Brest Canal was constructed in the 19th century.

Located in the centre of the Morbihan department, Josselin is a great place for outdoor recreation. Josselin is only 80 km (50 miles) west of Rennes, but it's a little off the usual route. It's also conveniently located just 55 kilometres (34 miles) west of the fabled Brocéliande woodland, which is home to Merlin's tomb for those with an interest in King Arthur.
The mairie (town hall; map), where helpful personnel may advise you on things to see and do in the town and its environs, is the source of tourist information for the little town of Josselin.

Tourist Information about Josselin: Mairie de Josselin de ROHAN Place Alain BP 36-56120 Josselin, France +33 (0)2 97 22 24 17.

Hotels:
When traveling, it's advisable to book your hotel in advance. I recommend using Booking.com for great deals, and it is available for some hotels in any country. Scan the QR code to learn more. Here are some recommended hotels to consider

- Hôtel du Château - Logis - 1 Rue du Général de Gaulle - Tel: +33 2 97 22 20 11
Relaxed riverfront retreat with views of the castle, a beautiful bar and a terrace restaurant.

- Hotel Rive Gauche - Address: 87 Chem. Glatinier - Phone: +33 2 97 75 63 36

Riverside elegance at 87 Chem. Glatinier, a restaurant with magnificent views and a blend of flavours.

- La Cour des Ursulines - 13 Rue Lucien Briend - Phone: +33 6 07 38 00 14

At 13 Rue Lucien Briend, you'll find a tranquil refuge with a 19th-century ambiance and personalised service in a one-of-a-kind environment.

- Relay De L'oust - Phone: +33 2 97 75 63 06 - Address: 16 le Rouvray en Forges de Lanouée Route Josselin Pontivy, D764

16 le Rouvray en Forges de Lanouée is a relaxed countryside getaway with comfortable rooms, patios, and canal views.

Festivals and Events:

Attending the events listed below in the city or nearby can make your trip memorable.

Josselin Mediaeval Festival
July 14:- Josselin's meeting location (every two years in even years).

Festiv'été: Summer musical entertainment every Wednesday.
ADEC56 Theatre Festival takes place on the third weekend of May.

"Weekends Chapel": Every weekend in July and August, the Holy Cross Chapel hosts a contemporary art exhibition, concerts, and shows. Meet the performers.

Mrs. Why How's City Tour:
A quirky figure, Mrs. Why How, guides you through the city of Josselin and his family history. During the summer, every Tuesday and Thursday.

Leisure Activities:
Here are some more activities and excursions in the city or nearby to get involved in:

- Cruise in the Gulf of Morbihan and its islands - 25 euros

Explore the Gulf of Morbihan, Ria d'Etel, and islands like Belle-Île-en-Mer with Navix, 39 kilometres from Josselin.

- Animal park La Ferme du Monde - 6 € to 9 €

Explore La Ferme du Monde, a 25-hectare wildlife park at Brocéliande with 400 animals, 37 kilometres from Josselin.

- A stroll on an antique rigging in the Gulf of Morbihan - Price: 40 € to 80 €

Sail on the Lys Noir, a sailing ship built in 1914, near Arradon, 43 km from Josselin, for a maritime adventure.

- A fun food-themed walk in Carabreizh World - Price: 0 € to 3 €

Discover Le Monde de Carabreizh in Landévant, 49 kilometres from Josselin, for an enjoyable self-guided tour from caramel to sweets.

Shopping:
While in the city, make sure to visit these recommended shops for a memorable shopping experience. You can bring back some souvenirs from your trip.

- Terre Enchantée - Type: Gift Shop - Location: 1 Place Notre Dame - Phone: +33 6 02 24 30 69

Terre Enchantée, located at 1 Place Notre Dame, offers beautiful goods. Open for in-store purchases.

- Au comptoir de Josselin - Type: Supermarket - Address: 2 Rue Olivier de Clisson - Phone: +33 6 82 09 24 82

Au comptoir de Josselin, located at 2 Rue Olivier de Clisson, is a grocery store where you may sample local flavours. There is in-store shopping accessible.

- COUTURE LUCIA - Type: Clothing store - Address: 8 Rue Beaumanoir Fashion treasures may be found at COUTURE LUCIA, which is located at 8 Rue Beaumanoir. Enjoy a pleasurable in-store shopping experience.

- Agnes Breizh - Address: 2 Rue Olivier de Clisson - Phone: +33 6 77 11 33 20 - Type: Fashion Accessories Store

At Agnes Breizh, 2 Rue Olivier de Clisson, you can accessorise with elegance. Open for in-store purchases.

- Merlin Biscuits - Ice Cream - Address: 1 Rue du Château

Merlin Biscuits, located at 1 Rue du Château, offers sweet treats.

Restaurants:

For a relaxed and enjoyable dining experience, try any of the following top restaurants. I've included their contact details:

- La Table d'O - Phone: +33 2 97 70 61 39 - Address: 9 Chem. Glatinier

La Table d'O offers French elegance with Coq au Vin and Escargot. Takeaway and dine-in options are available.

- LA TAVERNE - Josselin Restaurant - 4 Place Notre Dame - Phone: +33 9 82 20 28 47

LA TAVERNE has a classic appeal and serves Bouillabaisse and Ratatouille. There are both dine-in and take-out options.

- Le Guethenoc Restaurant - 11 Place Notre Dame - Phone: +33 2 97 70 69 57

Local flavours are highlighted at Restaurant Le Guethenoc, which specialises in Breton Galettes and Moules Frites. Takeaway and dine-in options are available.

- LA DUCHESSE ANNE - Address: 8 Place Duchesse Anne - Phone: +33 2 97 22 22 37

LA DUCHESSE ANNE, noted for its Bouillabaisse and Crêpes, combines tradition with innovation. There are both dine-in and take-out options.

- Crêperie La Sarrazine – 51 Chem. Glatinier – Phone: +33 2 97 22 37 80

La Sarrazine Crêperie serves real Galettes and Tarte Tatin. No delivery, only dine-in.

- La Terrasse - Phone: +33 2 97 22 20 35 - Address: 55 Chem. Glatinier

La Terrasse welcomes you with the best of Brittany, featuring a Breton-style Seafood Platter and Far Breton. No delivery, only dine-in.

Vannes

Vannes, a thriving city of 50,000 inhabitants, is centred around the port de plaisance, or marina, and the historic town centre.

The Place Gambetta, at the head of the port, is home to numerous restaurants, and the small port is dotted with boats. Through the Porte St-Vincent, you can also access the old city from Place Gambetta.

Wander along the ramparts to see different perspectives of the town, the walls, and the beautiful Jardins des

Ramparts (Ramparts Gardens). There are also several intriguing historic wash houses to see.

Beautiful, well-preserved antique homes may be seen as you stroll about the historic town. The buildings on the Place Henri IV date back to the sixteenth century. La Cohue Musée des Beaux-Arts, or the Fine Arts Museum, is located in the neighbouring Cohue, or marketplace, which is well worth seeing. Across from the museum lies the Cathédrale St-Pierre, which houses the tomb of Saint-Vincent Ferrier.

The edifice from the 16th century that features two carved and painted wooden busts is arguably the most distinctive feature of the old town. They've been dubbed "Vannes et Sa Femme" and it's assumed that they were a component of a shop sign.

Vannes is located 64 kilometres (40 miles) south of Josselin and about 30 kilometres (19 miles) northeast of Carnac. The distances between Quimper (117 kilometers/74 miles to the north west) and Rennes (115 kilometers/71 miles to the north east) are roughly equal. There are many options for an alfresco meal by the port, and the area is great to stroll around.

Check out on other cities in France

Quai Eric Tabarly, 56000 Vannes, France is the address of the tourist information centre. Phone: +33 2 97 47 24 34.

Hotels:

When traveling, it's advisable to book your hotel in advance. I recommend using Booking.com for great deals, and it is available for some hotels in any country. Scan the QR code in the first pages to learn more. Here are some recommended hotels to consider

- Hôtel Escale Oceania Vannes - Av. Jean Monnet - Téléphone: +33 2 97 47 59 60

This hotel is a good choice for guests in Vannes because of its simple rooms, free WiFi, and on-site restaurants.

- Hotel Kyriad Prestige Vannes - 36 Rue des Grandes Murailles - Tel: +33 2 30 30 83 08

A trendy and comfortable ambiance is created by streamlined rooms with complimentary Wi-Fi, a workout area, and a piano bar.

- Hôtel le Bretagne - Address: 36 Rue du Mené - Téléphone: +33 2 97 47 20 21

With its pleasant accommodations, Hôtel le Bretagne provides a friendly refuge, making it a charming choice in Vannes.

- Hôtel Kyriad Vannes Centre-Ville - Address: 8 Place de la Liberté - Phone: +33 2 97 63 27 36

This hotel is a sensible alternative in Vannes because of its casual rooms with free Wi-Fi, classic location, and convenient meeting space.

- PADJA Hôtel & Spa - 12 Rue Henri Navier, Zone Commerciale Vannes Ouest Parc Lann - Phone: +33 2 97 69 57 90

PADJA Hôtel & Spa provides a calm vacation in Vannes with discreet rooms, a relaxing spa, a pool, and a cafe.

- Best Western Plus Vannes Centre Ville - Address: 6 Place de la Liberté - Phone: +33 2 97 63 20 20

The Best Western Plus Vannes Centre Ville is a refined and modern hotel with balcony rooms, a restaurant, a bar, and complimentary Wi-Fi.

Restaurants:

For a relaxed and enjoyable dining experience, try any of the following top restaurants. I've included their contact details:

- Le Vieux Port Restaurant - Location: 26 Rue du Port - Phone: +33 2 97 47 93 93

In a quiet setting near the harbour, Le Vieux Port serves classic French cuisine such as Coq au Vin.

- La Tête en l'air Restaurant - 43 Rue de la Fontaine - Phone: +33 2 97 67 31 13

In a beautiful setting, La Tête en l'air delivers delicious Haute French delicacies such as Ratatouille.

- Le Tandem - 13 Rue des Halles - Téléphone: +33 2 97 63 53 37

Le Tandem encourages you to savour French specialties, including regional dishes such as Galettes in a welcoming atmosphere.

- Le Vent d'Est - Phone: +33 2 97 01 34 53 - Address: 21 Rue Ferdinand le Dressay

Le Vent d'Est invites you to a vintage-style restaurant serving nostalgic regional dishes including Crêpes.

- Chez La Mère 6 Sous - Address: 11 Rue Thomas de Closmadeuc - Phone: +33 2 97 01 93 67

Chez La Mère 6 Sous serves country-style foods such as Breton Stew.

- Le sous-sol Restaurant - 15 Pl. Maurice Marchais - Phone: +33 2 97 47 69 82

Le sous-sol serves imaginative meals in a modern setting, including local favourites such as Seafood Casserole.

Festivals and Events:
Attending the events listed below in the city or nearby can make your trip memorable.

- Arvor Festival - August 2024 - Location: Vannes - August 2024 - Vannes comes alive in August with a large folk gathering that fills the squares, streets, and ramparts.

- Lorient Interceltic Festival - August 2024 - Lorient, France

In August, Lorient celebrates variety and customs with a magnificent festival that offers an immersion into Celtic cultures.

- Les Escales - August 20, 2024 - Saint-Nazaire holds a festival that combines modern and traditional world music to create a lively, international musical experience.

- La Gacilly Photo Festival - July/August/September/October 2024 - Location: La Gacilly

The biggest open-air photo festival in France takes place in La Gacilly and runs from July to October, offering months of visual narrative.

- European Museum Night -: held throughout France

- Time: 2024 May

Experience a joyous evening of learning at museums throughout France on May's European Museum Night.

Leisure Activities:
Here are some more activities and excursions in the city or nearby to get involved in:

- Take a cruise around the islands and Gulf of Morbihan

- Cost: 25 euros - Distance from Vannes centre: 2.3 kilometres

Discover the islands and the Gulf of Morbihan with South Brittany's cruise specialist, Navix. Savour the outdoors and the ocean.

- Take an Old Rigging stroll on the Gulf of Morbihan - Cost: 40 to 80 euros - Distance: 7.1 km from Vannes

Sail in Arradon on the French sailing ship Lys Noir, built in 1914. Take a sailing adventure with a heritage label and experience nature.

- An enjoyable trail with a culinary theme in the World of Carabreizh - Cost: 0 to 3 € - Location: Landévant, 30 km from Vannes

In Landévant, take a delightful self-guided food-themed trail around Le Monde de Carabreizh. enhance your stay.

- Classes in drawing, painting, and three-dimensional art; cost: 15 €; location: Erdeven, 30 kilometres from Vannes

Take art classes in Erdeven to unleash your creativity in a refurbished setting near the outdoors.

- Take a tour of the Salt Marsh Workers' House Museum and Saltworks. Cost: 6 to 10 euros. Location: Guérande, 47 kilometres from Vannes

Discover the functioning of the salt marshes and the life of Paludiers by touring the Maison des Paludiers museum.

Shopping:

While in the city, make sure to visit these recommended shops for a memorable shopping experience. You can bring back some souvenirs from your trip.

- Carrefour Shopping Centre - Shopping Mall - Zone de Fourchêne, 95 Avenue de la Marne - Phone: +33 2 97 62 17 79

Carrefour Shopping Centre offers a diverse shopping experience, including in-store shopping and pick-up options.

- Kerlann Avenue - Shopping Mall - Location: Av. de la Marne

Kerlann Avenue, a retail centre on Av. de la Marne, offers in-store shopping.

- The Bretagne Boutique

- Address: 4 Rue Saint-Vincent - Phone: +33 2 97 42 58 65 - Type: Boutique

Discover one-of-a-kind things at La Boutique de Bretagne on Rue Saint-Vincent.

- Les Cop's - Address: 7 Pl. Lucien Laroche - Phone: +33 9 71 47 80 61 - Type: Clothing Store

Les Cop's on Pl. Lucien Laroche offers in-store shopping, pick-up, and delivery services, as well as fashionable bargains.

Roscoff

Located roughly 28 kilometres/ 17 miles northwest of Morlaix, in the Finistère area of Brittany, sits the little harbour town of Roscoff.

Regular service is offered by Brittany Ferries between Roscoff and Plymouth, England (about 10.5 hours) and Cork, Ireland (approximately 14 hours).

However, spend some time exploring Roscoff and soaking in its stunning surroundings. The Tourist Information Office may be reached at +33 2 98 61 12 13 and is situated on the Quai d'Auxerre, right close to the Phare (Lighthouse). They have maps and useful pamphlets that describe walking excursions in the town.

What to See
An extremely low tidal view of the town of Roscoff, with every boat beached. On the left, next to the lighthouse, is the Tourist Office.
A few churches, Roscoff's historic cannons and defences, the Vieux Port (Old Port), several exquisite old houses, the charming Chapelle Sainte-Barbe (constructed in 1619), and the Maison des Johnnies are among the sites to see. Breton labourers and farmers known as the "Onion Johnnies' ' went door-to-door across Britain, especially in Wales, selling the pink onions grown in the area. They were well recognised in Great Britain, riding their bikes and wearing striped Breton marinières. The area is still well-known for its red onions, even though hardly many are grown there anymore. Every summer, there is an onion festival!

Roscoff Saint-Barbe
The gorgeous Sainte-Barbe Chapel. From this peak, there are lovely views of the coast and Roscoff.
The Port de Plaisance de Roscoff, the marina, is also conveniently located if you're close to the ferry port. A few tiny eateries provide alfresco lunches while seeing the small boat activity, or, as it happened the day we visited, the rolling fog! La Hule, located near the port, served us a delicious lunch of fresh fish.

Trips Away from Roscoff (Excursions)

From Roscoff, you can go on a number of excursions. The small island right off the shore, Île de Batz, was our intended destination for the small boat, but sadly, the dock was being rebuilt the day we visited, so there were no boats.

Usually, the boat voyage takes only fifteen minutes, and once there, there are lots of options for hiking, beaching, and botanical garden visits. There are a few spots to camp and stay the night, but you'll want to make reservations in advance.

There are boat trips from Roscoff to the Baix de Morlaix as well. During this two-hour journey, you'll pass by various islands, including le Château de Taureau, and witness stunning cliffs, waterfront residences, and an abundance of birds. A visit to the Château is included in a separate 3-hour excursion.

The neighbouring town of Saint-Pol-de-Léon, which is well-known for its chapel and the Chapelle du Kreisker, is easily accessible by car.

Carantec is a historic little beach resort and spa town. You can walk to one of the several islands that are visible from here, but only during low tide.

Hotels:

When traveling, it's advisable to book your hotel in advance. I recommend using Booking.com for great deals, and it is available for some hotels in any country. Scan the QR code in the first pages to learn more. Here are some recommended hotels to consider

- Brittany Hotel & Spa

The home is upscale and located directly across from the beach. Reputable restaurant and spa with an indoor pool. +33 2 98 69 70 78, 22 Bd Sainte-Barbe,

- Mercure Roscoff Bord de Mer Hotel

Colourful rooms with views of the channel. Waterfront property with two bars. 27 Pl. Lacaze Duthiers can be reached at +33 2 98 61 24 95.

- Hotel D'Angleterre Rustic rooms in a low-key establishment. Restaurant with a relaxed atmosphere, a courtyard, free WiFi, and bike storage. +33 2 98 69 70 42, 28 Rue Albert de Mun.

- Hotel Armen Le Triton: Relaxed atmosphere, free parking, and Wi-Fi. Garden and terrace. +33 2 98 61 24 44, Rue du Dr Louis Bagot.

- Roscoff Hotel Le Temps de Vivre

In a stone mansion, a refined beach hotel. Simple quarters, some with balconies. 19 Pl. Lacaze Duthiers can be reached at +33 2 98 19 33 19.

Festivals and Events:
Attending the events listed below in the city or nearby can make your trip memorable.

Market Day (Weekly): Roscoff offers a colourful market every Wednesday, exhibiting local produce and crafts.

Onion's Get-Together Roscoff: A savoury cultural event, Roscoff's legendary onions are celebrated annually after August 15.

Legacy Days: Held on the third weekend of September, Heritage Days provide a glimpse into Roscoff's rich cultural and historical legacy.

Tango Festival by the Cote: From late July to early August, immerse yourself in the passion of tango while enjoying breathtaking views of the shore.

Pardon of Sainte-Barbe: This religious celebration honours Sainte-Barbe and brings residents together in reverence on the third weekend of July.
Nearby Festivals
- Old Plough Festival (Carhaix-Plouguer): July 2024, a four-day feast of music and revelry that will rank among Europe's best.

- World's End Festival (Crozon): August 2024, a multicultural music refuge at the confluence of varied worldwide sounds that promises a one-of-a-kind musical journey.

- Brest International nautical Festival (Brest): In July 2026, see a massive gathering of vessels in Brest harbour, a fantastic spectacle for nautical aficionados and bystanders.

Leisure Activities

- Roscoff Exotic Botanical Garden: Explore "The Southern Hemisphere in Northern Finistere" at this 16,000-square-kilometer garden located 1.6 kilometres from Roscoff's centre. Prices range from €3 to €6.

- Kerlouan Musical Tour: Take an outdoor musical excursion through Meneham village, 29 kilometres from Roscoff. Price: €17.

- Alidade Sailing offers sea fantasies in the Abers (Landéda) at Aber Wrac'h, Landéda, 45 kilometres from Roscoff. Prices begin at €210.

Restaurants:

For a relaxed and enjoyable dining experience, try any of the following top restaurants. I've included their contact details:

- Le Bistrot de la Mer - Address: 4 Rue Amiral Réveillère - Phone: +33 2 98 69 72 03

Coastal appeal and a seafood paradise. Try the Bouillabaisse, which is famed for its freshness and rich flavours.

- L'Ecume des Jours - Phone: +33 2 98 61 22 83 - Location: Quai d'Auxerre

By the quay, enjoy elegant French cuisine. Enjoy Coq au Vin, a sophisticated take on a classic meal.

- La Moule Au Pot – 13 Rue Edouard Corbière – Phone: +33 2 98 19 33 60

A nice location for mussels and other seafood. Enjoy a Galette Saucisse, a Breton speciality.

- Chez Janie - Phone: +33 2 98 61 24 25 - Address: 8 Rue Gambetta

A seafood resort on the beach. For a taste of the sea, try a Plateau de Fruits de Mer.

- Le Surcouf Brewery - 14 Rue Amiral Réveillère - Tel: +33 2 98 69 71 89

Brewery with a nautical flair. Pair your beer with a traditional Breton crêpe.

Shopping:
- Balen L'échoppe De L'océan - Category: Home Goods - Address: 11 Rue Gambetta - Phone: +33 2 98 72 96 59

Find seaside treasures for your home. Everything from nautical decor to kitchen necessities is available.

- Horizon Roscoff - Clothing store - Address: 25 Pl. Lacaze Duthiers Fashion finds with a view. This beachfront boutique offers fashionable apparel.

- SiouxSie - Type: Women's Clothing Store - Location: 11 Rue Gambetta - Phone: +33 2 98 79 38 80

Women's fashionable styles. SiouxSie provides handpicked clothes with an elegant touch.

- Comptoir Mers et Montagnes - Address: 11 Rue Amiral Réveillère - Phone: +33 2 98 72 90 29 - Type: Clothing store

Fashion inspired by the water and the mountains. Discover one-of-a-kind clothing that combines seaside and alpine influences.

- LES GOURMANDISES DE LUCETTE - Grocery store - 29 Rue Amiral Réveillère - Phone: +33 2 98 69 78 25

Gourmet treats are on the way. Lucette's grocery store is a paradise for gourmet foods and local delicacies.

Carantec

Carantec is a small seaside village located 14 kilometres (9 miles) north of Morlaix and 17 kilometres (11 miles) southeast of Roscoff. It is a popular summer destination. In addition to tourism, it has a big oyster cultivation sector. If you haven't experienced Breton oysters yet, Carantec is a terrific place to start!

Visitors to Carantec frequently visit the Château du Taureau. Built to safeguard Morlaix from British invasion, it is now accessible via boat. Boats leave from Roscoff, Carantec (plage du Kelenn), and Plougasnou (port du Diben).

The château is a castle erected between the 16th and 18th centuries. It has functioned as a defence fort, a prison, a vacation residence, and even a sailing school over the years! It was decaying in the 1980s, but it was saved and may now be visited. It exists as an island and is sometimes referred to as Brittany's Alcatraz. Le Taureau means "the bull," and the builders intended it to be aggressive and powerful.

Carantec Château du Taureau
The fog had lifted enough to allow us to view Île Louet and the Château du Taureau.
Morlaix was a prosperous community beginning in the 16th century, mainly to the commerce in linen and hemp. Its strategic location at the mouth of the English Channel was also significant. It was vital to safeguard it!

The Île Callot is another attraction in Carantec. This small island is located close off the coast of Carantec and has various small bays, dunes, fields, and other features. Historically, it was an area for fishing, farming, and seaweed collection. It now has 17 year-round residents and is famous for its granite and potatoes.

Because the causeway is only accessible at low tide, visiting Île Callot needs some forethought. When we arrived in Carantec, it was nearly high tide, and Callot was plainly an island, with no means to reach it by car. A big sign warned travellers and displayed the tide table. Tides in this region can be tremendous, as anyone who has visited Mont-Saint-Michel or St-Malo can attest. Pay attention to the warnings!

The black section in the front is the causeway that leads to Île Callot, but because it was close to high tide, it was clearly impossible to walk there.
There are various hiking routes in Carantec that lead down to beaches or to locations with good views of the Château du Taureau, Île Callot, or Île Louet and its lighthouse. Eight of the chapelet d'ilots islands form a bird reserve. It is well-known for tern nesting.

Be warned that fog is typical along this coast. In fact, when we initially arrived in Carantec, it was completely fogged in, and it appeared as if there was nothing out in the lake. After a few minutes, it began to clear, and shortly Voila! We could see Île Louet and the Château du Taureau. So, if you don't see anything, just wait a few minutes! Take pictures as soon as you see the islands!

In June 1940, Charles de Gaulle visited Carantec to take his family, who had been vacationing there, before departing for England.

Tourist Office Address: 4 Rue Pasteur, 29660 Carantec, France Phone: +33 2 98 67 00 43

Hotels:
When traveling, it's advisable to book your hotel in advance. I recommend using Booking.com for great deals, and it is available for some hotels in any country. Scan the QR code in the first pages to learn more. Here are some recommended hotels to consider

Hôtel La Baie de Morlaix, The Originals Boutique
17 Bis Rue Albert-Louppe | Phone: +33 2 98 67 07 64
Breakfast is served in a little stone building. The charming apartments provide a peaceful refuge with a touch of elegance.

Chambres d'hôtes et villas de position Vue Mer Carantec
The address is 7 Imp. de Kerliezec | +33 6 63 12 99 45
Secluded B&B with a sea-view balcony. The open dining room and relaxed atmosphere create a cosy beach hideaway.

Carantec Logis Hotel
Phone: +33 2 98 67 00 47 | Address: 20 Rue du Kelenn
Comfort and style come together. The Logis Hôtel de Carantec provides a classy stay with a dash of local flavour.

Stella Maris
Phone: +33 6 68 27 95 94 | Address: 13 Rue Lamotte Picquet
Stella Maris is a seaside haven. Despite its simplicity, it appeals to people seeking a peaceful escape by the sea.

Kerélec
Phone: +33 6 68 27 95 94 | Address: 13 Rue Lamotte
Picquet
Kerélec is a coastal jewel. It promises an intimate escape
with only four rooms, merging modern luxury with
beach tranquilly.

Festivals and Events:
Attending the events listed below in the city or nearby
can make your trip memorable.

- Exhibitions at the Winter Fair:
- Carantec is the location.
- December dates
Professional artists display a variety of works,
encouraging artistic expression in the wonderful winter
setting.

- Summer Events at Les Soirées Transat:
- Locations include the Jardin du Verger, Kelenn Beach,
and Callot Island.
- Schedule: Mondays through Thursdays (July 14
through August 15).
A colourful summer series in various scenic locations
offering storytelling, theatre, music, dance, movie,
sports, and family programmes. Admission is free.

- Callot's Weekly Market at the Passage:
- Callot is the location.
- Weekdays: Thursdays

Discover the region's varied gastronomic options at the Thursday morning market, a hub for discovering the local terroir.

- Cornish Festival:
- Place: Quimper
- July 20, 2024

Immerse yourself in Quimper culture by attending a unique festival that celebrates art and the local way of life.

- Festival of the Old Plough:
- Carhaix-Plouguer is the location.
- July 20, 2024

For four days of jubilant festivals, music, and cultural revelry, join the European-famous Old Plough Festival in Carhaix-Plouguer.

Leisure Activities:
Here are some more activities and excursions in the city or nearby to get involved in:

- Musical Tour in Rustic Brittany:
- Price: 17 €

Explore the history of the Meneham location, 34 kilometres from Carantec, with a singer-guitarist who will lead you through the musical tale of the ancient village.

- Sailing Adventure in the Abers:
- Price: 210 €

Set sail with Alidade Sailing from Aber Wrac'h, Landéda, in Finistère. With specialised programmes, you may make your marine ambitions a reality.

Restaurants:
For a relaxed and enjoyable dining experience, try any of the following top restaurants. I've included their contact details:

- The Table of Ty Pot
5 Place de la République | Phone: +33 2 98 69 80 08
La Table de Ty Pot is a French elegance where culinary expertise meets classics like Coq au Vin.

- Le Cabestan
Phone: +33 2 98 67 01 87 | Address: 7 Rue du Port
Le Cabestan, a waterfront treasure, welcomes you with Bouillabaisse and a view that compliments every dish.

- Le Relais
Phone: +33 2 98 78 30 03 | Address: 4 Plage du Kelenn
Le Petit Relais is a beachfront paradise. Crêpes and fresh seafood delicacies capture the heart of Brittany.

- Ty Brizec Crêperie Restaurant
5 Place de la Libération | Phone: +33 2 98 67 04 93
Crêperie Ty Brizec, where Galettes and Cidre come together to provide a genuine Breton experience

- Les Retrouvailles
Phone: +33 2 98 78 31 03 | Address: 2 Plage du Kelenn

Les Retrouvailles is a gastronomic reunion. Each taste, from strawberries to seafood, offers a delectable narrative.

Shopping:
- Concept Store LA PASSERELLE

Type: Shop | Location: 10 Rue Albert-Louppe | Phone: +33 2 98 67 65 23
LA PASSERELLE, a concept boutique on Rue Albert-Louppe, features a carefully curated range of one-of-a-kind products.

- Léon de La Ménardière Gallery

Home products store | 9 Rue Amiral Ronarch | Phone: +33 6 67 17 64 61
Amiral Ronarch is graced with Galerie Léon de La Ménardière, a mecca for home decor enthusiasts.

- Casino Store

Type: Supermarket | Location: 2 Imp. Parc Coz rue Du | +33 2 98 67 92 69
Casino Shop, a convenient supermarket, greets visitors to Imp. Coz Park is located on Rue Du.

- Espace Loisirs Carantec

Sporting goods store | ZA de Kerinec | Phone: +33 2 98 67 92 55
Carantec Espace Loisirs at ZA de Kerinec, where sports enthusiasts can find high-quality equipment and gear.

- The Isle of the Dames

1 Rue Maréchal Foch | Phone: +33 2 98 67 49 69 | Type: Gift shop
On Rue Maréchal Foch, L'Île Aux Dames, a beautiful gift shop, awaits with delightful items.

Brest

Finistère translates as "land's end" or "end of the earth," and Brest, perched on the coast at the far northwestern edge of Brittany, can appear far away. But it's only 71 kilometres (44 miles) from Quimper, and TGV trains from Paris can take you there in as little as five hours.

Although Brest has a lengthy history, little of it has survived due to its strategic location and intense bombing during World War II. The waterside Château offers a look into the past.

When you first see the harbour, you'll understand why Brest has been so vital for so long: it's a broad, sheltered bay shielded from Atlantic storms—and from attackers—by the Crozon Peninsula, which is located well "inland" from the point of the peninsula.

Oldies (Brest)
Brest also has a significant maritime history, dating back to 1631 when Cardinal Richelieu designated it as a military harbour. The Château de Brest, the gigantic harbour guardian that has existed here in some form for 1700 years—the oldest castle in the world continually in military use—is one of the city's two most notable surviving historic buildings. The Tour de Tanguy, located across the channel from the château, was built in the mid-1300s. It now houses the Brest History Museum.

During World War I, it was a vital port for American troops and supplies en route to France to aid the Allies. The occupying German navy built an important submarine facility here during WWII, in addition to the port's other uses as a naval harbour and shipbuilding site.
It is now France's second-largest naval port (behind Toulon). The city's lifeblood is maritime commerce.

Transportation
Train
TGV trains go in as little as 3-1/2 hours between the Gare de Brest SNCF and Paris-Montparnasse, and in

little over two hours between Brest and Rennes. To obtain the fastest train, make your reservation in advance.

Brittany's cities and towns are linked by Breizhgo TER regional trains and buses (cars in French).

Airport

Brest Bretagne Airport (BES; sometimes known as Brest-Guipavas) handles internal French flights as well as international flights to and from Ireland, Greece, Morocco, Portugal, and Spain.

Bus Intercity

By bus, Eurolines, Flixbus, and Ouibus connect Brest to other European locations.

Transportation by Public

City Buses, Trams, and Cable Cars

Bibus manages Brest's municipal transport system, which comprises city buses, a tram line and the cable car (téléferique) that connects Boulevard Jean Moulin on the east bank of the River Penfeld with the Ateliers station on the west bank.

Ferries

Penn Ar Bed, the Breton title for Finistère, is also the name of the ferry company that connects Ouessant, Molène, and Sein.

Brest Ouest (or Le Brestoâ) operates a ferry service between Brest and the Crozon peninsula, as well as harbour excursions.

Information for Tourists
The friendly Office de Tourisme de Brest Métropole may be reached at +33 2 98 44 24 96 and is located in the city centre at 8 avenue Georges Clemenceau near the Place de la Liberté.

What to See

As previously said, Brest is a huge and sophisticated city. There are wide boulevards to wander along, such as the avenue de Siam and the massive Place de la Liberté. The city centre is located on a hill, and the stroll down to the port area is enjoyable. Walking back up is a little more difficult!

As you ascend up, you will notice a tall red granite monument with a view of the harbour. The inscription reads, "Erected by the United States of America to commemorate the achievements of the Naval Forces of the United States and France during the World War." It was built after World War I, destroyed by the Germans in 1941, and restored in 1958. It was an important boarding station for the American Expeditionary Forces in 1917-18 because it was France's westernmost port.

There are various seafood restaurants in the port area, as well as excursion boats that give tours of the inner harbour as well as longer cruises to Camaret on the Presqu'Île de Crozon or further out to several islands off the coast.

There are several museums worth visiting in town, including the National Marine Museum, which is housed in the château and focuses on Brest's maritime history;

the Museum of Fine Arts, whose collection of paintings, sculptures, and graphic arts reflects the city's marine culture; and the Tour Tanguy.

The Tour Tanguy is located in the Recouvrance area, which means "recovery" or "safe return to port." Recouvrance, a working-class, Breton-speaking district, with a distinct identity and a lengthy history.
The tower itself is thought to date from the 14th century and was part of the defences that ensured or impeded connection between the two sides of the Penfeld River. It is right across from the Château and provides wonderful views of that landmark.

The Tour Tanguy was purchased by the city of Brest in 1954, and it currently serves as a museum of Brest history, Musée du Vieux Brest. Dioramas depict significant historical events in the city.
The sellers at the magnificent open air market on the rue de Lyon demonstrate Brest's multicultural and global population today. On a Sunday, we went, and it was a vibrant scene, with stalls selling Breton specialties as well as Brazilian, Arabic, African, and other foods. In addition, vendors sold clothing, leather goods, home goods, and other items.

Speaking of food, this region of Brittany is famous for its excellent strawberries, many of which come from the Plougastel Peninsula, which is located approximately 15 minutes east of Brest. We visited in June and took full use of the wonderful offerings.

Hotels:

When traveling, it's advisable to book your hotel in advance. I recommend using Booking.com for great deals, and it is available for some hotels in any country. Scan the QR code in the first pages to learn more. Here are some recommended hotels to consider

- Oceania Brest Centre Hotel
- Address: 82 Rue de Siam
- Phone: +33 2 98 80 66 66

A modern treasure with polished rooms, seafood delights and a lively bar that provides a perfect blend of comfort and sophistication.

- Centre Brest Logis Hotel
- Address: 4 Bd Léon Blum
- Phone: +33 2 98 80 78 07

A down-to-earth hideaway with a restaurant, spa, and free parking, guaranteeing a peaceful vacation with all the necessities.

- Kyriad Brest Centre Hotel
- Address: 157 Rue Jean Jaurès
- Phone: +33 2 98 43 58 58

Relaxed hideaway with modern rooms, free Wi-Fi, a bar and a fitness area that caters to leisure and convenience.

- Brest Hotel Restaurant L'Amirauté
- Address: 41 Rue Branda
- Phone: +33 2 98 80 84 00

For a laid-back stay, this casual charmer with Wi-Fi offers basic rooms, a restaurant and a bar.

- The Bellevue Hotel
- Address: 53 Rue Victor Hugo
- Phone: +33 2 98 80 51 78

Low-key refuge with modest rooms, TVs, and free Wi-Fi, as well as breakfast and convenient parking.

Leisure Activities:
Here are some more activities and excursions in the city or nearby to get involved in:

- Sailing Trip in Abers
- Discover the water with Alidade Sailing in Landéda, 24 kilometres from Brest. Live your seafaring dreams alone or with family starting at €210.

- Rustic Brittany to the Sound of Music Musical Tour
- For €17, visit Meneham in Kerlouan, 31 kilometres from Brest. Discover this mediaeval village with the help of a singer-guitarist.

Festivals and Events:
Attending the events listed below in the city or nearby can make your trip memorable.

The Brest Thunders: Every four years, the city organises the Brest Maritime Festival, which brings together vessels and sailors from all over the world for a week of cultural sharing and exchange in joy and kindness.

The Port Thursdays: A summer highlight on the Commerce waterfront, under the banner of festival, sharing, and fun! The sea and music are the stars of the show! Thursdays at the Port aren't only for music; there are plenty of events and activities for both adults and children. Street theatre, concerts, but also traditional games and circus arts are available in space on Thursday nights during the summer in Brest.

Astropolis Festival: Astropolis has established itself as a major electronic music event in France. Mega concerts are staged in the port of commerce in August, and electro clubs succeed in the afternoons and evenings, giving a taste of the massive electro concert that will close the festival, held in wood Keroual.

The Brest Metropole Oceane presents the European Short Film Festival of Brest each year, with the goal of revealing the talent that will fill the theatres tomorrow.

The Atlantic Jazz event: During this event in the autumn, numerous local, national, and worldwide performers animate the city! This is an opportunity to marvel at new music's virtuoso talent as well as its quality and originality.

The dull sound of snare drums, the might of the bomb, and the symphony of bagpipes rang through the streets of downtown Brest this spring. Without a doubt, it heralds the arrival of Spring! Every year in May, the stunning procession of bagadoù, down the street Jean Jaures fanfare, is a spectacle. This event provides an opportunity to showcase Breton culture in all of its splendour and legend.

Shopping:
While in the city, make sure to visit these recommended shops for a memorable shopping experience. You can bring back some souvenirs from your trip.

Brest Iroise Commercial Centre
- Shopping centre
- Location: 126 Bd de Plymouth
- Phone: +33 826 25 32 35

Espace Jaurès (Coeur de Jaurès) - Commercial Centre
- Shopping centre
- Location: 65 Rue Jean Jaurès
- Phone: +33 2 98 46 02 57

The Gallery - Europe's Phare
- Shopping centre
- Location: 29 Rue de Gouesnou
- Phone: +33 2 98 42 07 25

Jack Square London
- Shopping centre
- Location: Pl. Mr. Jack London

Carrefour Market Commercial Centre
- Shopping centre
- Location: Pl. Emperor Napoleon III
- Phone: +33 2 98 03 00 60

Restaurants:
For a relaxed and enjoyable dining experience, try any of the following top restaurants. I've included their contact details:

- The Four Winds
- Address: 18 Quai de la Douane
- Phone: +33 2 98 44 42 84
From savoury seafood platters to substantial steak meals, this seaside café serves the best of Brittany.

- The Ocean's House
- Address: 2 Quai de la Douane
- Phone: +33 2 98 80 44 84
Enjoy harbour views while dining on specialties like moules marinières and bouillabaisse at this coastal resort.

- Peck and co.
- Address: 23 Rue Fautras
- Phone: +33 2 98 43 30 13
A vibrant restaurant serving a broad menu ranging from conventional crêpes to regional specialties such as kouign-amann.

- Bretonne Jaurès Embassy
- Address: 70 Rue Jean Jaurès
- Phone: +33 2 29 62 08 36

With galettes, cider, and traditional Breton pleasures, this crêperie showcases Brittany's culinary appeal.

Dinard

Dinard, situated on the west bank of the expansive River Rance and across from St-Malo (located on the east bank), was primarily developed as a resort by affluent Americans and British in the late 1800s. Along the coast, many of their Victorian mansions are still intact.

Dinard's many wide beaches and pleasant climate make it a popular destination for vacationers, especially British ones. It holds the Festival of British Films every October.

Saint-Malo and the Emerald Coast can be seen from walks along the beach. Even at low tide, when the sea is otherwise far away, one can swim in a sizable enclosed saltwater pool. Check the tides before leaving, as some walkways may be submerged during high tide.

Transportation:
Dinard and St-Malo are frequently connected by ferry during the summer. There may be irregular service during the off-season. Regarding specific sailings, check with the Tourist Information Office. From Dinard, you can see St-Malo and its ramparts or check my book on Saint-Malo.

The majority of Dinard's stores, eateries, and lodging are located in the vicinity of the town's main beach, the Plage de l'Ecluse. The town's 19th-century villas are primarily located in the Pointe de la Malouine to the west of this location; to the east are the port and Pointe du Moulinet, both of which make for enjoyable exploration.

Even though Dinard's town centre is smaller than we anticipated for such a significant resort, it still has a nice selection of cafes and some interesting stores. Place de la Republique is home to the tourist office, while Rue Levasseur and Boulevard du President Wilson are the main shopping areas.

Summertime at Dinard beach
Head to the broad promenade behind the main beach to begin your visit to Dinard. Along the seafront, there are some of the best examples of 19th-century houses, and the views of the sea are pleasant.

If the weather isn't perfect for the beach, you can always go shopping in the town centre, which is home to a huge variety of stores, cafes, restaurants, and boutiques. We also had a great time touring the Dinard center's art galleries, and we were happy to discover that some of them featured pieces that had nothing to do with the sea!

Dinard's Plage de l'Ecluse is home to a striking statue of Alfred Hitchcock, which was erected in honour of the town's 20th annual film festival. There doesn't seem to be any proof that Hitchcock visited the town or used a Dinard villa for Psycho or Birds, despite a lot of claims to the contrary.

Dinard's shoreline and beaches

In addition to other lovely sandy beaches nearby, the town boasts a number of pleasant beaches that serve as the beginning point for lovely walks along the coastline. The Plage de l'Ecluse is the primary beach in the heart of Dinard and offers the greatest amenities and activities. The beach is made more charming by the white and blue-striped beach huts.

The most impressive villas can be found at the Plage de Saint-Enogat and Plage Port Riou, which are located west of the Pointe de la Malouine. A little further west is the Plage de Port Blanc, which is less developed but generally quieter than the beaches in the centre. The Plage du Prieuré is a different beach located south of the Pointe du Moulinet.

Adjacent to the beach at the easternmost point of Plage de l'Ecluse is a spacious circular pool that is highly frequented by tourists.

Dinard town centre
To make sure you see the most impressive mansions and monuments, we advise you to ask for the map of the town at the Dinard tourist office.

You'll notice several other noteworthy structures in Dinard, most of which are made of the local granite. These include the impressive Manoir de la Baronnais, which dates from the 17th century, the charming little ancient priory, and the Maison du Prince Noir, which dates from the 14th century.

Rue Levasseur ends at the port for Dinard, from where you can see Saint-Malo, which is a short distance away, as well as the Plage du Prieuré and the sea.

There is a sizable rose garden and a kids' play area in Port Breton Park, which is located across from the Prieure beach. Dinard has a casino, just like a lot of other French beach resorts.

There's a market every morning in the Halles de la Concorde, and there's one in Place Crolard on Tuesdays, Thursdays, and Saturdays. There is also an antiques and vide grenier market in Dinard, which is held every Sunday from early April to early September at the Esplanade de la Halle.

Explore Around Dinard

Dinard was the place to go to see the rich and famous and was regarded as France's top seaside resort by the end of the 1800s. Dinard is therefore home to many lovely villas, many of which are now protected buildings due to their distinctive and eclectic styles. The best way to view these is to explore the Pointe du Moulinet and the Pointe de la Malouine.

Paths enveloping the Pointe du Moulinet and the Pointe de la Malouine run parallel to the coast in both directions. The "Moonlight walk," also known as the "Promenade du Clair de Lune," is a great stroll that winds through the gardens between the Pointe du Moulinet and the beach at Prieure. The gardens are illuminated at night and feature live music.

Further villas can be found along the Pointe de la Malouine, and stunning views of St. Malo across the water can be had from the Pointe du Moulinet. There are other walks that explore the area surrounding Dinard if you are staying for a few days. These include the Pointe de la Vicomte, which is along the coast further south, and Saint-Enogat, which is to the west of the town.

Dinard hosts regular markets every Wednesday, Tuesday, Thursday, and Saturday.

Hotels:

When traveling, it's advisable to book your hotel in advance. I recommend using Booking.com for great deals, and it is available for some hotels in any country. Scan the QR code in the first pages to learn more. Here are some recommended hotels to consider

- Le Grand Hôtel Dinard - 46 Avenue George V - Phone: +33 2 99 88 26 26
    Elegant accommodations, regal dining, a spa, and an indoor pool. Enjoy water views in opulent surroundings.

- LES ALIZÉS DINARD HOSTEL
    - Address: 11 Pl. de Newquay - Telephone: +33 2 99 16 87 27
    A relaxed hotel in a historic building. There are modern rooms, Wi-Fi, and a comfortable lounge.

- Hôtel du Parc - Dinard - Phone: +33 2 99 46 11 39 - Address: 20 Av. Edouard VII
    Relaxed rooms in a century-old hotel. Enjoy an informal bar in a relaxed setting.

- Dinard Balmoral Hotel - Address: 26 Rue du Maréchal Leclerc - Phone: +33 2 99 46 16 97
    Hotel with unassuming rooms, free WiFi, optional breakfast, and afternoon tea.

MGallery - Royal Émeraude Dinard - 1 Bd Albert 1er - Phone: +33 2 99 46 19 19
    Elegant seaside hotel from 1892 with sophisticated rooms, a bar and spa treatments.

- Hôtel Saint-Michel - Dinard - Phone: +33 2 99 73 81 60 - Address: 54 Bd Lhotellier

Family-run hotel with relaxed rooms, a garden and a bar. Wi-Fi is provided for free.

Leisure Activities:

Here are some more activities and excursions in the city or nearby to get involved in:

- Crossing from Dinard to Saint-Malo on a Vedette boatDinard's nature and great outdoors

8 €

We invite you to explore the North Brittany Coast: Crossings of regular lines: Saint-Malo / Dinard, Ile Cézembre, Iles Chausey. Coastal cruises discussed: Saint-Malo Bay, Cap Fréhel Château de Fort La Latte, Dinan and the Rance Valley, Cancale.

Dinard's centre is 300 metres away.

- Ride a Segway to get a different perspective on Saint-Malo.

Saint-Malo entertainment

29 € to 45 €

Gyromalo takes you on a playful and original tour of Saint-Malo and its surroundings. You will discover unexpected places, and Sylvain tells you stories about Malouine history that he is passionate about.

Dinard is 2.8 kilometres away.

From Pointe du Grouin to Cap Fréhel, take a private cruise.Saint-Malo's nature and great outdoors

160 € to 400 €

The Emerald Coast was mentioned during sea walks. Boat privatisation, maximum of 7 people.

Dinard is 2.1 kilometres away.

- Cruise with commentary in Saint-Malo Bay. Saint-Malo culture and education

23 €

Visitors have been allowed to discover the Emerald Coast from the sea since 1904. Regular crossings: Saint-Malo / Dinard (every 20 minutes), Ile Cézembre, Iles Chausey. Coastal cruises discussed: Bay of Saint-Malo, Cap Fréhel Château de...

Dinard is 2.6 kilometres away.

Festivals and Events:

Attending the events listed below in the city or nearby can make your trip memorable.

Dinardese cultural programmes are rich and diverse, displaying all the scores of the live show, all the colours and suggestions of art combined with science, all the sounds of music:

The association Musiques Errances organises a jazz concert with the city of Dinard on the last Friday of each month.
Easter weekend: an antiques show.
In April, there will be a festival of young fashion designers.
Estivales of laughter in May.
In June, visit the gardens.

From June to September, the Palace of Arts and Festival hosts a large art exhibition.

Summer exhibition at the Villa Roches Brunes, organised by Dinard's heritage department, from July to September.
Summer operas take place in July.

Two pyrotechnic and musical shows in July and August.

Heritage is held in July and August. Tours of the city of Dinard's theatres are organised.

Summer theatrical season takes place in July and August.

International Music Festival in August.

In August, there will be an evening of gallery openings and artist workshops.

Nature in Celebration, Brittany's most important ecological event, takes place in Port Breton Park in September.

European Heritage Days are held in September.
Dinard British Film Festival, first weekend of October.

Festival du Film Britannique
Dinard will host an exceptional showcase for British cinema in October

Nearby Festivals
Normandy hosts an eclectic jazz festival.
From May 4 to 11, in Coutances

Nightfall Festival is a one-of-a-kind, multi-disciplinary event held in Rennes in July

La Route du Rock is an independent music festival held in Saint-Malo, France, in August

Trans Musicales Rennes Festival
An excellent location for observing and discovering the best of the international music scene.
Rennes, France, from December.

Marathon de Mont-Saint-Michel
A one-of-a-kind marathon in one of the world's most beautiful locations
Cancale, May, Mont-Saint-Michel

Shopping:

While in the city, make sure to visit these recommended shops for a memorable shopping experience. You can bring back some souvenirs from your trip.

- St. James
  - Category: Clothing Store - Location: 37 Rue Levavasseur - Phone: +33 2 30 32 12 27
  - Shopping: in-store purchases and in-store pickup

- Comme des Garçons
  - Category: Clothing Store - Location: 2 Rue du Maréchal Leclerc - Phone: +33 6 81 25 84 48
  - Shopping: Shopping in a store

- Armour Lux
  - 35 Rue Levavasseur - Phone: +33 2 90 57 20 48 - Type: Clothing store
  - Shopping: Shopping in a store

- CAPITAL MARINE
  - Category: Clothing Store - Location: 43 Rue Levavasseur - Phone: +33 2 99 88 11 98
  - Shopping: Shopping in a store

Restaurants:

For a relaxed and enjoyable dining experience, try any of the following top restaurants. I've included their contact details:

- L'Escale à Corto - 12 Avenue George V - Phone: +33 2 99 46 78 57

French cuisine with a Brittany twist. There will be no takeaway or delivery.

- Didier Méril Restaurant - 1 Pl. du Général de Gaulle - Phone: +33 2 99 46 95 74

Elegant French restaurant with comfortable rooms. Enjoy regional specialties such as Breton seafood.

- Pourquoi Pas Dinard - Address: 17 Av. George V - Phone: +33 2 99 80 30 00

Haute French cuisine with breathtaking bay views. Breton gastronomy offers elevated cuisine.

- Vents et Marées - 66 Bd Albert Lacroix - Tel: +33 2 99 16 48 74

French cuisine with a seaside twist. Dine in or order takeaway to enjoy seaside flavours.

- Le Cancaven - 3 Place de la République - Phone: +33 2 99 46 15 45

The atmosphere is that of a brasserie. A bustling spot with traditional Brittany dishes and a lively atmosphere.

General information (France)

Electricity

French Plugs and Sockets: French plugs and sockets are hermaphroditic, which means that both the plug and the socket have prongs. This is unique to France and requires adapters for international visitors.

Voltage and Hertz: France utilises 220-240 volts and 50-60 Hertz, thus check the voltage compatibility of your gadgets. Most current electronics can withstand voltages ranging from 100 to 240 volts.

Adapters: To fit into French sockets, use multi-adapters that accept various plug types. Smaller adapters may not have the ground/earth prong.

Extension cables & 3-Socket Cubes: Keep extension cables and 3-socket cubes on hand for easy access to electrical outlets, particularly at hotels.

Charging Station: To accommodate several devices while travelling, set up a charging station with power cord splitters or power strips.

Be Wary of Surge Suppressors: Do not use North American surge suppressors in France since they may not be able to manage the 240-volt, 50-Hz current. Instead, look for basic power strips.
Extension wire: Carry a 1- or 2-meter extension wire with you to position your charging station easily in places with limited outlet access.

Wi-Fi and Network

Most hotels in France provide Wi-Fi, while more expensive hotels frequently charge for it. When you check in, request the Wi-Fi password.
For more security, consider using a Virtual Private Network.

Transportation

Train: For regional and high-speed transport, SNCF operates a comprehensive rail network that includes Transilien, TER, Intercités, Ouigo, idTGV, and TGV inOui trains.

Plane: Airlines such as Air France, EasyJet, and regional carriers connect major cities.

Car: Car rental is an option, with adequate highways but possible tolls. In Paris, avoid renting.

Parking: Multi-level parking lots with clearly marked prices are prevalent. Some require chip-enabled credit cards, and smartphone apps such as Flowbird are used.

Ship & Ferry: English Channel ferries connect England and Ireland to Normandy and Brittany ports.

Bus: There are city, municipal, regional, national, and international bus systems, which are frequently co-located with rail stations. Bus routes inside France and to other countries are provided by companies such as Eurolines and Flixbus.

Best time to visit

The best seasons to visit France are spring (April to early June) and fall (late September to mid-November).

Summer is pleasant (mid-June to mid-September), but winter (mid-November to March) can be dreary and frigid. Events can be plentiful in February, March, April, June, and September.

Currency and Money Exchange

Many travellers are unconcerned about currency conversion rates. This might significantly increase the cost of their journey.

To avoid unfavourable exchange rates and high costs, I used Wise (TransferWise), which provides international electronic banking and currency exchange at competitive prices.

I opened a Wise account, transferred funds from my bank to it, and then converted the funds to euros as needed using the Wise smartphone app or website. Transfers and payments are instant (unlike banks, which might take days). Fees are minimal or non-existent.

I also ordered a Wise Debit Card, which can be used to pay for products or withdraw cash from an ATM just like any other bank debit card. I save money because Wise debits our account in the currency of the purchase, eliminating the need for a currency exchange charge or fee.

More Money exchange ideas

Exchange money once you arrive in France, as currency exchange offices are becoming increasingly scarce. Withdraw cash in euros from ATMs.

- For a better value, consider purchasing leftover euros from friends at the interbank exchange rate.

- To avoid unfavourable airport exchange rates, keep some extra euros from prior visits to utilise at the start of your next journey.

- If you're taking a taxi from the airport, stop at an ATM in the city centre to get euros.

- Use credit or debit cards for the majority of transactions, especially those with no foreign exchange fees, and avoid using cash.

Money-saving advice

- No Tipping: In France, a service charge is included in the costs of hotels, restaurants, and cafes, therefore tipping is not required.

- Save at Café-Bars: If you're only interested in beverages, stand at the counter/bar instead of sitting at a table.

- Pack a Picnic: Pack a picnic for lunch or dinner because French cheeses, bread, wine, and other foods are great and inexpensive when purchased in stores.

- Formule or Menu: When dining out, choose set-price meals or the daily special plate (plat du jour) since they provide fresh and excellent selections at a lower cost than à la carte goods.

- Le Pichet Magique: Many restaurants offer inexpensive house wine; you can have a glass (verre) or a carafe (pichet) of wine, which can be a good value.

- Train Tickets: Purchase your tickets online because French railways use pricing techniques that can result in varying fares for the same seats. Purchasing tickets in advance is advised to avoid last-minute problems.

- Métro Tickets: In Paris, buy Métro tickets in a carnet (a set of ten tickets) to save roughly 20% on the price per ticket. Weekly transit passes are also available.

Communication

There are three options for remaining connected in France International roaming from your home phone provider.

- While international roaming is convenient, it can be costly.
- A French phone company's short-term phone service.

French phone provider plans are less expensive, but you will have a French phone number.

- An MVNO "Wifi Everywhere" service that does not include regular phone service. MVNOs are inexpensive, but you won't have a standard phone number and will have to rely on data apps for communication.

Considerations for MVNO "Wifi Everywhere" services include:

Using data-only MVNOs with apps such as WhatsApp, Skype, and others.

Check that your smartphone is unlocked and eSIM-compatible.

Set up an MVNO account and payment before arriving in France, but keep in mind that you will not be able to receive calls to your home number.

Although many French MVNOs provide low-cost data plans, they may be subject to restrictions.

Registration for a French SIM/eSIM and phone number is required:

- Within 30 days, register with the French government.
- Provide your full name, French address, SIM/eSIM number, and ID.
- Your MVNO or major phone operator may be able to assist you with registration.

In conclusion, choose the choice that best meets your communication needs and budget in France, taking into account the trade-offs between convenience, cost, and having a traditional phone number.

Apps you must have for your vacation to France:

Waze provides real-time traffic updates.
Google Maps provides extensive navigation.
Transportation: Use **Citymapper** to find the most effective public transportation routes.

Fuel: **Gas Now**, looking for nearby petrol stations.
Google Translate is available for linguistic assistance.
Restaurant recommendations can be found at **The Fork**.
Tiqets are used to purchase last-minute tickets.

Uber is a convenient mode of transportation.
France Weather app that provides local forecasts.
Currency: For exact conversion rates, use the **XE currency converter.**
Flush to locate the nearest public bathrooms.
Stay connected with **Whatsapp, Facebook, Gmail, Hotmail, Yahoo, Instagram, Skype**, and **Viber**.
TouchNote for mailing physical postcards from your phone.

What to Wear in Different Seasons
Summer in the city can be hot and humid, so wear light cottons during the day and a jumper or jacket at night.

In the spring and autumn, bring a jumper, jacket or topcoat, as well as an umbrella. Scarves are currently popular in Paris, particularly during these seasons.

Winter weather can be quite cold and chilly, with little sunlight, so you'll need woollens.
Rain can fall at any time of year.

Travelling on your own schedule offers for a more personalised and bespoke experience.

When arranging your trip, keep these in mind.

Learn about the destination's top attractions, local culture, and activities. To learn more, contact the Tourist Office.

Make a Budget: Decide how much money you're willing to spend on transportation, lodging, meals, and activities.

Make a Timeline: Determine how many days you will spend at your location and create a daily agenda.

Always reserve your accomodation ahead of time. Check that they are in a handy location for your planned activity.

Transportation: Arrange transportation to and from the destination, whether by plane, train, or auto rental.

Budget travel to France:

Flights: Round-trip tickets vary (451 to 725 EUR) based on location, season, and airline.

Accommodation: Budget hotel/hostel costs (32 to 62 EUR per night), totaling (61 to 121 EUR) for two nights.

Transportation: One-way tickets (1.91 to 2.42 EUR), 3-day total (22 to 32 EUR).

Food and drinks: Dining in cheap restaurants (11 to 21 EUR per meal), 3-day total (91 to 151 EUR).

Sightseeing: Some attractions are free or have nominal fees, while others may cost (51 to 101 EUR) for three days.

A 2-night, 3-day trip on a budget can range from (251 to 451 EUR), but actual costs depend on your preferences and activities.

Help leave positive reviews and check out other cities in France by the author. "Hudson Miles"
There is a France travel guide written by me titled "Current France- Exploring France with the essential travel information (Travel Guide)"
Check the current information in France.
Safe travels

Scan the QR code below and search for the Location you are going to in France and have a better view. Safe travels.

The map is the same on your phone. Consider taking screenshots as you walk around with no connection needed. Alternatively, you can contact the tourist office using the addresses and numbers provided in this guide.

Write down your plans and activities in the box below

Day 1	Day 2	Day 3
Arrival (hotel) and Acquaintance	Adventure (leisure) and relaxation	Explore and Farewell

Write down your plans and activities in the box below

Day 4	Day 5	Day 6
Arrival (hotel) and Acquaintance	Adventure (leisure) and relaxation	Explore and Farewell

In most cases, I use the Wanderlog website or app to plan my trip itinerary and expenses. You can try it if you're interested. Click the link below or scan the QR code to create a new account.

https://wanderlog.com

Notes

Self-Reflection questions

Traveling to Brittany offers the chance for personal development in addition to stunning scenery and fascinating cultural experiences. You can improve your trip experience by reflecting on yourself, obtaining new perspectives, and making enduring memories. Before and after your trip, use the following questions to help you with your introspection.

Prior to Departure:

Take time to consider your expectations as you get ready to travel to Brittany. How may your experience be shaped by these expectations?

_____

_____

_____

_____

_____

_____

_____

_____

_____

- Think about the significance of the locations you have selected in Brittany. Why are you drawn to these locations? Are there any particular historical or cultural facets that pique your interest?

_____

_____

_____

_____

_____

_____

_____

_____

_____

Examine your perspective on lodgings. Which would you prefer—comfort, immersion in the area, or a combination of the two? How might the lodging you choose affect how you feel about the vacation as a whole?

_____

_____

_____

_____

_____

_____

_____

_____

_____

- Consider your chosen mode of transportation for the trip. Are you more drawn to the convenience of flying, the efficiency of trains, or the picturesque routes of a road trip? How might your choice of mode of transportation affect the story of your trip?

_____

_____

Think about whether you're willing to take a risk before leaving. Are you willing to embrace unplanned excursions, interact with locals, and try new foods? In what ways do you think this transparency will help you grow personally?

_____

_____

_____

_____

_____

_____

After your trip

Review your pre-trip plans. In what ways did your experience's actuality match or diverge from these preliminary ideas? What understanding have you received regarding the significance of controlling expectations when travelling?

_____

_____

_____

_____

_____

_____

_____

_____

_____

- Consider the accommodations you selected. What effect did the decision have on your entire experience? Did it make you feel more a part of the community or did it offer a place to unwind?

_____

_____

_____

_____

_____

_____

_____

_____

_____

- Reflect on the most enjoyable times you had while travelling. Which encounters, locations, or activities stand out as the highlights? How can you make these happy places a part of your everyday routine back home?

_____

_____

_____

_____

_____

_____

_____

_____

_____

- Consider any difficulties or unpleasant experiences you have while travelling. What lessons did you learn from conquering these obstacles, and how did you handle them? How can you use these principles to overcome obstacles in your daily life?

_____

_____

_____

_____

_____

_____

_____

_____

_____

_____

Examine how your perspective has changed as a result of cultural immersion. How has being involved with the people, cultures, and traditions of the region influenced your perception of Brittany? How might you incorporate these fresh viewpoints into your larger perspective?

_____

_____

_____

Printed in Great Britain
by Amazon

42439706R00096